THE SOPHISTICATED SAVAGE

By

Carla Seidl

The Sophisticated Savage. Copyright © 2009, Carla Seidl.

All rights reserved.

No part of this book may be reproduced in any manner whatsoever without written permission, except in the case of brief quotations embodied in critical articles and reviews.

Cover Design and Photo by Carla Seidl, Background Image iStockPhoto

www.thesophisticatedsavage.info
www.carlaseidl.com

ISBN: 978-0-578-01334-3

Library of Congress Control Number: 2009923352

First published in the United States of America in Huntington, New York by Inner Hearth Books, 2009.

With thanks to Fredy, for his openness, generous spirit, and life teachings.

THE SOPHISTICATED SAVAGE

CONTENTS

1. Introduction (Two Journeys to the Equator)   1
2. In Search of the Primitive   27
3. The Ladder of Civilization   59
4. Leaving the Tribe   73
5. Between Worlds   89
6. Casanova Surfer   99
7. Island Life   113
8. Without Need   123
9. Tigers and Anacondas   127
10. Jungle Surfing   135
11. Lobería Legend   141
12. Reflecting on Two Worlds   147
13. Amazon Bound   155
14. Tasting *Chicha*   163
15. Adventures in Tena   173
16. Crêpe Talk   181
17. Digging Up Dirt   185
18. Tying the Vines   195

Epilogue   199
Bibliography   217

Introduction
(Two Journeys To The Equator)

I come from advanced civilization. I attended one of the most prestigious universities in the world, I have had my own car, and I have never gone without food. Shouldn't I and others like myself feel happy with our lives? Yet we don't—there seems to be something missing, and more and more, it seems as though young people from privileged backgrounds are searching for that something in less developed areas of the world, where we think things are simpler. And coming from a hyper-complicated world, simpler seems like it must be better.

I met Fredy in 2001 on the Galápagos island of San Cristóbal. He was a surfer called Billabong known to have a way with the girls, and I was a nineteen-year-old volunteer English teacher from Harvard. Our steps and styles were far apart, but on the dance floor, they matched. Fredy taught me to enjoy dancing with a partner, and I taught him that the same moves do not work for everyone. In September of 2005, I returned to the Galápagos with the idea of writing a book about Fredy's life.

San Cristóbal Island, Galápagos, Ecuador

July 2001

The music in the *discoteca* Neptuno is loud and pulsing through my body, music of a type I never knew existed, but to which my body says, yes, here is some earth I can crumble and sift through my hands, scrunch between my toes. Dig into and move with, off beat with the flashing lights that move in fleeting waves across my eyes.

Fredy sits pressed against me, his arm around my shoulders. Through his shirt I can feel the hardness of his chest and I note the calluses on his hand holding mine. I look around to see if anyone is watching us, and notice some furtive glances in our direction. The new *gringa*[1] meat for Fredy, some might be thinking, but I am not too bothered, only a twinge of—wait, what am I doing?—white prudish respectability.

Fredy is a good dancer, and true to his word, a first-rate teacher of salsa and merengue. An island in the Pacific, a surfer boyfriend, no one I know—this taste of another life makes me feel free and refreshed.

Fredy leans into my ear and says in his stuttering speech that at first turned me off, "Q-Q-Quiero decirte algo." I want to tell you something.

"Sure," I respond.

"In the jungle, where I come from, I was a cannibal."

My eyebrows shoot up, and my eyes bulge so that Fredy quickly continues, "B-but d-don't worry, I'm not going to eat you." We laugh. Way to break the tension. I come back, "Did I tell you I'm a vegetarian?"

---

[1] *Gringo* (feminine, *gringa*) is a Spanish term used to refer to foreigners. In most parts of Latin America, gringo refers to white-skinned foreigners, usually from the United States, and has a derogatory connotation.

The author with sea lions on a Galápagos beach, 2001

In the summer of 2001, I left the United States for the first time. Burned out from competitive academia and suffering from feelings of social isolation after my sophomore year at Harvard, I planned an entire year away, the first part of which was to teach English for two months in the Galápagos Islands of Ecuador as a volunteer with the program WorldTeach. I received a grant from the David Rockefeller Center for Latin American Studies to cover half of the costs, and paid the other half from my savings from birthday gifts and part-time work.

My placement was, as I requested, relatively removed from the other volunteers: I was assigned to teach on the island of San Cristóbal, in the capital town of Puerto Baquerizo Moreno. San Cristóbal, despite holding the capital, is a lot more tranquil and less frequented by tourists than the larger island of Santa Cruz, and this relative peacefulness and isolation greatly appealed to me.

My host family on San Cristóbal consisted of my host mother, Mercedes Segura, her fifteen-year-old daughter, Jessica, her sixteen-year-old niece, Nancy, and, for much of my stay, Mercedes' boyfriend Rubén, who was a lawyer on the island. As I was only nineteen at the time, I became both a role model and friend to Nancy and Jessica, especially Nancy, who was more into swimming, snorkeling, and dancing than beauty and boyfriends. I had a private room in the small house, and Mercedes ran an ice cream shop next door, where she sold twenty-one flavors of Zanzibar-brand ice cream that she had shipped over monthly from the mainland by boat. There in the ice cream shop, Mercedes prepared a grilled cheese sandwich along with a *batido*, a fruit and milk shake, for my breakfast and dinner. At lunch, the only time the others ate, Nancy and Jessica came back from school and we all sat down to a large meal of soup, white rice, and chicken or fish with a sugary drink mixed from powder.

Host home and ice cream shop, San Cristóbal

Mercedes often talked with me about wanting to leave San Cristóbal Island. She had grown up in Quito and had worked for the phone company for a number of years there, and she finds San Cristóbal to be lonely and isolating. She tells me that she does not like to cook, and asks me with envy whether it is true that in the United States, you can buy all of your food from the supermarket already prepared so that all you have to do is heat them up. Well, yes, I tell her, but those are not very good quality or good for you; I tell her that I prefer to cook everything from scratch. She looks at me as if, why would you want to do that? Mercedes says that she flew to Las Vegas once to visit a friend and she was so impressed with the city—she wants to live there! Whereas for me and most tourists and volunteers, the Galápagos is a paradise that given the chance and the presence of friends and family, they might never want to leave.

I taught five English classes on the island that summer: one for the National Park employees, two for middle schoolers in a local school, one for preschoolers, and one that I helped organize and that became my most enjoyable and rewarding, to community women, mostly fishermen's wives, in the evenings. With my schedule relatively full with teaching, plus the various times I was in bed, sick from the food and water, I did not have that much free time, but still much more than I was used to in the United States. After my afternoon run, I would go down to Playa Mann, the beach just a stone's throw away from my house, to swim, read, and, often, watch amazing sunsets. It was here that I met Fredy, a person who would have a major impact on my life.

First Encounter

I was heading back across Playa Mann to Mercedes' house when I was startled to hear a voice calling in a British-accented English, "Hello there, would you care to join us for a round of cards?" I looked over and saw a young, moderately heavyset blonde woman with a friendly disposition holding a cigarette and shuffling after me in the sand. I was caught. "Oh, well, sure," I replied with more than a hint of hesitation. I am not one eager to chat or socialize with strangers, but as one of the few white and English-speaking young people on the island, it would have looked terribly unfriendly, I realized, to refuse this invitation. Reluctantly, I followed the *gringa* to her spot in the sand, where she introduced me to her Ecuadorian boyfriend and another Galápagos dweller, a surfer named Fredy. Fredy asked me if I spoke Spanish, and seemed super impressed to learn that I did. I, meanwhile, was put off both by the stutter that became apparent in his speech and by his interest—all the Ecuadorian men I had met, so far, seemed excessively interested in talking and flirting with me.

Fredy told me about his surfing and invited me to eat dinner that evening at the Hotel Orca, the fanciest one on the island, where he was a cook. I declined, saying that I had to teach my women's English class at the Estación Charles Darwin. Another time, he said, better sooner than later. I laughed politely, and excused myself, thinking, "My God do these men have nerve."

Each day for days after, I would see Fredy at the beach or *por la calle* while walking home from my evening women's class. And each time we met, Fredy invited me to go out with him. Eventually I gave in, admiring his determination and thinking that he seemed like a nice enough guy, despite his seemingly superficial interest in me and his stutter, which I found decidedly unattractive.

Walking with Fredy by the *muelle* one evening, I learn that "Billabong," the name everyone calls him, comes from the surf-oriented clothing line company of that name, which sends him free Billabong-brand clothes ever since he sent them a picture of himself surfing. I look again and realize that Fredy does seem like he could be physically attractive—although barely medium in height, he has a nice, chiseled body and a rather cute face with a dimple in his chin. We pass by one of the two *discotecas* on this street and he asks me if I would like to go inside. "Do you like to salsa?" I tell him I don't know how, and that I don't like following steps. He does not back down. "I master teacher," he assures me, "Lesson, free of charge."

Fredy and his surfboard, 2001

True to his word, Fredy is a wonderful dancer—from what I can tell, the best on the island. Even though I usually prefer individual, free form, spontaneous dance to following steps, it is not torturous to dance salsa with Fredy because his movements flow very naturally, and he guides so well that I can concentrate on the feeling of the dance rather than the form. Giovanny, a good-looking friend of Fredy's, watches us dance together and whistles, impressed. He comes over to slap Fredy on the back and congratulate him on finding a *gringa* who can dance.

After the *discoteca*, we go to Scuba Bar, a cute bar on the main strip where the tourist boats come in. Here, Fredy and I make a winning foosball, called "minifoot" team. He knows how to get the ball where he wants it to go. He has so much control over his actions, yet such spontaneity! Still, when Fredy asks me to be his girlfriend, I find myself hesitating. I have heard from my host sister Nancy about what a player Fredy is, always after the foreign girls. Plus, I don't feel a whole lot of understanding between us apart from on the dance floor. I explain to Fredy that I am a serious person, interested only in serious relationships, and that no, I don't think I want to be his *novia*. It does feel nice to be pressed in close to Fredy's hard, muscled body, though.

When I see Fredy a couple of days later, he brings me music cassettes to listen to as well as a white chocolate bar. I protest these gifts, and also his compliments, like *dulce para la dulce*, sweet for the sweet, but he deals with my cynicism very well. He says he has been thinking about me a lot, but I don't believe it. I'm sure he has the mind of a player. Still, his persistence is charming and wears down my cold edges. I am flattered by his interest, and going out with him is a fun way for me to get to know the island culture better.

We go out for the next couple of weeks, and while I do not feel like I can connect with Fredy intellectually, nonetheless there is definitely a strong connection between. He leans me up against a big statue of a sea lion and says that he's considering going to work on a boat in the coming weeks. Do I want him to go? No, I say, truthfully. And yet, I am not obsessed with Fredy, like I have been with others in the United States. I just enjoy being with him. Fredy has a certain magnetism and warmth that spreads from his body to mine, making me feel content. He is like the sun, or a warm blanket, yet very much alive and excited about things.

Over a bottle of Inca Cola one day, "my cola," he jokes, because he says he is a descendant of the Incas, Fredy tells me more about his past. "I was born on the mainland of Ecuador," he says, "in the jungle region called the *Oriente*. My father was king of our tribe, and I was chosen to be the next king. The night before I was supposed to get married, though, I ran away." Fredy tells me that he came to the Galápagos about six years ago, not speaking any Spanish. He is not properly documented by the Ecuadorian government, he explains, because the government does not keep birth records of remote jungle tribes. Fredy used to work as a guide in the jungle, and kept a pet parrot.

"My parents? I do not know what they are doing now...." When I ask him what his parents do in the jungle, he explains that people do not go to work there as they do here—there is no work there, just survival. "There was no music or dance there, either;" Fredy says, "I learned how to dance when I got to the Galápagos." I am impressed, but think that Fredy's amazing dance abilities must have something to do with his being especially tuned into natural rhythms from his jungle past.

Walking back to my host mother's house after the *discoteca* one night, Fredy stops to kiss me. He puts his hand on my breast, and suddenly I feel like I want to melt into that very spot with him, not resist any more. One night soon after, Fredy invites me to come back to his room with him, a small apartment in a hotel by the beach. Despite the dim lighting, I see a mattress on the floor, and pictures of scantily clad models and surf pictures plastering the walls. He is passion. Hard and knowledgeable in that energy, a vibrant arrow, coordinated and direct, his thrusting, so rapid, demanding, unrestrained. Later, lying on the mattress, Fredy says, "We created fire tonight." Naively, I ask him, did he come? And he looks confused and says yes. Have I done this before, he asks. No, I say. He doesn't believe me at first, but then looks at me like I have given him something special, that I must feel very strongly about him. An hour later, I am almost asleep when Fredy says he is going out to a party. "Do you want to come?" he asks. "Huh?" I say, exhausted, "No."

Nancy tells me that Fredy is with a new white tourist or volunteer every couple of weeks. I play down our relationship, as Mercedes, my host mother, also seems to think Fredy is not a serious person. I feel that she looks down on him for being indigenous. When I ask her whether she herself is indigenous, she seems offended, as though of course I should be able to tell just by looking at her that she has Spanish blood, not native blood. For me, there is no difference. She tells me that there are other indigenous people here on the island, and, during a parade of all the island residents, she points them out to me, a group getting no fanfare and looking bedraggled, marching at the very end. Fredy, in his fashionable clothes, does not look like them at all.

My relationship with Fredy continues for the rest of the summer. Always generous and caring, when I return from a trip to the island of Santa Cruz hobbling around on a twisted foot, Fredy goes and buys me DencoRub, a clear substance in a tube for me to rub on my foot to relieve the pain. I am very busy teaching and preparing for my five classes, so the two of us really don't spend a lot of time together. When we are together, though, he makes me feel special. He actually has me worried that he cares a lot more for me than I do for him. Our major connection comes at night, at the *discoteca*, where Fredy and I dance crazily together, crazy in a wonderful, coordinated way. Our turns are fast and sharp and varied, and there is no end to the different motions we create. When we salsa and merengue, Fredy does lead, but for some reason, this does not bother me; I feel the energy behind his choices of movements and approve of them; I want to follow them because he is a great dancer and they are what I, too, want to do.

    I am very interested in finding out more about Fredy's past and we have several interesting conversations about his life in the jungle. It bothers me, though, that Fredy does not seem to be particularly interested in what I might have to tell him. Often, he acts as though he already knows what I am about to tell him and interrupts me, which is really irritating. Fredy has never heard of Harvard, and it seems like he is not interested in what people in the United States usually like about me, such as my insights or musical abilities. Besides the fact that I am a good dancer, I don't understand what Fredy likes about me. Just my looks and the possibility of sex?

    My journal in late July shows my conflict: "It is really weird for me to feel that someone so interested in me has no idea about or means of understanding or appreciating what are usually considered my talents—singing, for example, or things intellectual....My attraction to Fredy, if I can call it that, is physical, more than anything, and this is refreshing in its difference for me."

The day before I left the Galápagos, the other WorldTeach volunteers came to San Cristóbal because we were all going to be leaving from the airport in my host town. At our farewell party, I felt very awkward having Fredy there with the volunteers I'd gotten to know during our teacher orientation in Quito, because two very different spheres of my life were colliding and I felt unable to act in both at the same time. I felt that, in the mindset of the highly educated, analytical-minded volunteers, and part of my own mind as well, my being with Fredy would make no sense, for I certainly would not go out with someone in the United States if we could not connect intellectually and if I did not feel like the person appreciated and understood me. When Fredy told me that he was going to come to the airport the next morning to say a final goodbye, I resisted, telling him that I didn't want him to—I felt like he couldn't fit into my U.S. world that included the other volunteers and my supervisor, who were leaving from the same airport. Luckily, Fredy knew enough to ignore my protests and came to the airport bearing flowers anyway.

When I returned to the United States, I told my friend Susan about my Fredy escapade. It seemed like such an adventure in the telling—losing my virginity to a cannibal? But more than a quick adventure, I found myself considering whether I might like to live in the Galápagos. In my reminiscence, I was so relaxed over there; I felt so much less inhibited than I do in the United States. For example, whereas in the United States I had not even kissed anyone, apart from performing in musicals, on the Galápagos, I had only been there a few weeks and had already had sex. In the United States, I mused, my romantic relationships would necessarily involve a lot of analysis and agonizing, whereas on the Galápagos everything was simple. Thinking of life there, I imagined watching lots of beautiful sunsets, dancing often and unrestrained, in tune with the life force, and being free from the confines of constant analysis. What would it be like to marry Fredy, I wondered. With such different gene pools, we would certainly have beautiful children together, and they would be adept at everything.

From Marianna Torgovnick, *Primitive Passions*:

> "...the West has tended to scant some vital human emotions and sensations of relatedness and interdependence....These sensations include effacement of the self and the intuition of profound connections between humans and land, humans and animals, humans and minerals, of a kind normally found in Europe and the United States only within mystical traditions."[2]

The following spring, when I left the United States for the second time to study abroad in Chile, I was most looking forward to an experience like the one I'd had in the Galápagos—finding a local boyfriend, enjoying a more relaxed pace of living, and dancing a lot. When I arrived in the capital city of

---

[2] Torgovnick, *Primitive Passions*, 4.

Santiago and found Chilean culture very frigid and not much different from the United States, with a lot of work and stress, little open friendliness, and people without rhythm for life or dancing, I spent a lot of time daydreaming about Fredy and going back to the Galápagos for a visit. I researched flights to go over there, but found that despite the relative proximity, it was a lot more expensive than flying there from the United States. I remember around this time telling my good friend and fellow study abroad student Lilia that I thought I was never going to be able to have sex in the United States because that culture repressed me too much.

Through the next weeks and months, the Galápagos became a symbol to me of the things that were missing from my life in the United States. I desperately wanted to integrate some of the Galápagos lifestyle I had experienced into my life, but I did not know how. Returning to Harvard, I felt less interested in the academic world than ever, and this isolated me from most of my classmates. And in the years that followed, I thought about Fredy and his way of life whenever my own environment was especially removed from his, more "natural" way of existence. If I felt inhibited from dancing passionately, for instance, or if I was involved in an overly analytical discussion, or if the web of car and health insurance and other "necessities" of advanced civilization made my head throb and my blood boil, sometimes I would hear Fredy's carefree laugh scoffing at me and my worries. Was the Galápagos the wonderful culture I made it to be in my mind, or was it just a dream that it was so great? In 2005, newly free from romantic attachment and wanting to explore an interest in documentaries, I decided to return to the Galápagos and find out more about Fredy's life.

September 2005

San Cristóbal Island is rocky and fairly barren near the coast, with a lush highland toward the center of the island. It is not one of the more wildlife-rich islands, but you can see a lot of *lobos marinos*, or sea lions, as well as pelicans, iguanas, crabs, and blue-footed boobies. The major town, Puerto Baquerizo Moreno, also the capital of the islands, was customized only minimally for tourists when I was there in 2001, with three *discotecas*, the Scuba Bar, and one place for karaoke, but by 2005 there had been many changes due to the construction of a university on the beach right next to my host mother's house. There is a fast food restaurant downtown now called Yogurt Persa, where they sell fried balls of *pan de yuca*, like potato bread, with cups of a sugary, milkshake-like, fruit flavored yogurt, along with personal pizzas and hamburgers. The university looks massive and out of place on the small beach and brings a lot more foreigners to the island.

Despite all of this development, the relaxed Galápagos culture seems to continue to thrive on San Cristóbal. As a local surfer named Giovanni tells me one day, "The tranquility you find here, you won't find anywhere else. It's so tranquil, that you can have a normal rhythm of life, where no one hurries you, no one tells you what you have to do, like that you have to go to a meeting at a certain hour....One day you surf, another day, you stay at home, another day you hang out by the pier, and take photos…it's great here!"

I emailed Fredy before buying my plane tickets to Ecuador to see what his schedule was going to be and if he had a girlfriend at the time who might not like it if I spent a lot of time with him. I was not sure if I had any romantic interest in Fredy, outside of the physical longing to dance with him again, so I explained to him, too, that I did not think I was interested in him romantically and asked if it would be all right with him if I did a lot of interviews with him and spent time with him just as a friend. Sure, Fredy wrote back, and that no, he was not going to be working, that he was on vacation, so he could spend as much time with me as I wanted. I did not really understand this—how could he have nothing at all to do, no schedule at all, for a period of three weeks to three months, which was how long I told him I was coming for?

Fredy had called me in the United States a few times after I left in 2001, once on Long Island and a couple of times when I was back at Harvard, but it was always hard for us to communicate. He would say oh, that yes, everything is great on the Galápagos, that he was going to various parties, and surfing every day, but except for these banal facts we didn't really have anything to talk about. I knew that he would not be able to commiserate, for instance, with my college stresses.

I called Fredy from Guayaquil the night before I flew to the Galápagos, as he wanted me to, to let him know what flight I was on (the airport on Santa Cruz, the major tourist island, was shut down for repairs so I was able to fly directly into San Cristóbal), and he said, "*Quiero correr contigo,*" literally, I want to run with you. I thought that must be some kind of expression for going out, that he was saying that he wanted me to be his girlfriend, so I tried to avoid the issue by saying that I didn't understand what he meant. When I finally realized that he meant that he wanted to run with me, for exercise, like he remembered me doing in 2001 in training for the Outward Bound program I was preparing for, I felt silly. This was definitely an instance of my overanalyzing things and his being simple and direct.

Second Encounter

I arrive at the airport on San Cristóbal, pay my $100 tourist entry fee, and am waiting for my baggage when I see a Nike hat and a pair of dark glasses pop up over the wall on the outside of the building. "Carla?" a voice in that direction says. "Yes." Fredy is there waiting for me. He easily calls to a nearby pickup truck and has it drop us off at his apartment, a tiny single room with a bathroom, partially divided by a half wall into a living room, consisting of a concrete bench built into the wall, and a bedroom with just room for the bed. Fredy has offered that I can stay with him if I want, and he says now that I can sleep on his bed, and he can take a long cushion out from under the bed and put it in the small floor space between the bench and the wall and sleep there. I tell him that I appreciate his offer, but ask to see a separate apartment he says he has found for me. He has told the landlord that I am coming to volunteer on the island, and she has agreed on a special, reduced price of ten dollars per night for a really nice room with a spectacular balcony view of the water and the town. On the one hand, I want to spend as much time with Fredy as possible, but on the other, I know that if I stay with him, he will try to put the moves on me every night, and I am not sure I want that and also want privacy to transcribe interviews and reflect on my project. The apartment turns out to be a wise choice.

View of Puerto Baquerizo Moreno from author's apartment

Newly arriving on the island, I take stock of Fredy—has he changed? Let's see…Fredy is solid and muscular, with a young-looking face, but shorter than I remember, maybe 5′6″ or 5′7″. He totes a cell phone and tells me that he goes to the gym sometimes to work out. I notice a huge barbell outside his door made of concrete poured around a pipe, which I can't lift even an inch off the ground. "Try these Oakleys," Fredy says. "I will lend them to you." He is wearing another pair, and tells me that they cost over a hundred dollars. For going to the bar at night, Fredy wears a Nike hat, a Columbia collared button-down shirt, and Reef pants. So fashionable! When we play pool, I see that he is really a champion. Without pausing to consider or calculate, he approaches the cue ball and bam! Knocks two or three of his balls in.

It turns out that I am only going to be in my rented apartment to sleep at night and to transcribe my interviews from the previous day early in the morning; Fredy was not kidding when he said he had no other obligations—we spend all day of every day together. I go over to his apartment, which is about a fifteen-minute walk across town from mine, at ten o'clock each morning. We hang out there in his room, listening to music and talking, for about forty-five minutes, and then we interview for about an hour, recording on my minidisc recorder. Then, we might dance for a while, or go to the Internet place before going to lunch at one of the local restaurants where Fredy always eats. After lunch, a hike up to *Las Tijeretas*, a rocky cliff with lots of birds called *tijeretas*, or to his surfing spot, then dinner, also at the local restaurant, then hanging out at a bar called Iguana Rock.

On the day of my first interview with Fredy, I take a closer look around his apartment and notice his surfboard stored above the ceiling beams. All my friends do that, Fredy says, because of the limited space. But what more do I need, Fredy points out—I have hot water in my shower! I used to have a stove for cooking, too, he says. Fredy has no kitchen in his apartment, I notice, but it actually works out better for him to eat out all the time, he explains, because on the Galápagos, the food items brought over from the mainland are quite expensive—for a single person, it is by far cheaper to eat out at one of the restaurants for locals than to buy all of the ingredients and cook for oneself.

Eating at the restaurants for locals is a new and interesting experience for me. There is no menu to look at; you simply go in and say whether you would like a whole meal or just a part of it. For lunch, you can order a complete *almuerzo*, which includes a soup course, often containing potato-like yuca, a starchy root vegetable that I find especially comforting, a *segundo*, consisting of rice with chicken, fish, or beef or a large meatball of various meats with peas and raisins inside, along with a miniature salad, a large glass of juice, and something sweet, like an orange, a banana, or a piece of cake. Or, you can have just the *segundo*, the rice, meat, and salad, with juice. For dinner, it's the same thing, but without the dessert—you can order a *merienda* with or without the soup. For these meals, the price is fixed and is between $1.50 and $2.50 (Ecuador uses the U.S. dollar now) depending on the restaurant and whether you order the complete meal or just the *segundo*. Perhaps the lack of menu turns the tourists and other *gringos* off, but the food is pretty good and definitely beats paying eight to twelve dollars for a meal at one of the tourist restaurants. While I don't normally eat meat, for instance, I like that everyone eats the same thing here, because it gives a feeling of community and connectedness. Plus, since everyone is ordering the same thing, you don't risk getting something really bad that the cook doesn't know how to prepare. Yet at the same time, people at these local restaurants usually watch TV as they eat, a habit that really detracts from my personal eating experience, and I am surprised to see that it is very common to eat alone there—often Fredy and I are the exceptions, coming in and eating together. People do look at us a little curiously, but I think they are used to Fredy coming in every few weeks with a new *gringa*.

While I don't think I'm just another *gringa* for Fredy, the status of Fredy and my relationship is unclear during the trip, especially after the massage that violates our supposed friend status by turning into him rubbing my breasts and pulsating against me with his clothes on, causing both of us to come. On the one hand, I long for the feelings of freedom and connectedness that came with dancing and physical intimacy with Fredy in 2001. But on the other, I now see that I am not particularly attracted to Fredy. I have become more connected with myself in the past years, and know more about what meshes well with my inner being and what does not. It is clear that Fredy and I are not connecting on mental and emotional levels that would be necessary for me to want to be in a romantic relationship with him.

"*Ven, ven a papi,*" Fredy always says to me, wanting me to lie down next to him. It is really nice to be in his arms, as they feel strong, warm, and generous, and I crave feeling cared for. Yet I cringe when he says *ven a papi*, as though I am a small, weak creature needing protection, or worse—a piece of meat. No, I say, and draw back. Ugh. Papi.

Still, when a French woman staying next door to me tells me, after watching Fredy and me dance together and observing both of our personalities, that she thinks Fredy and I make a great couple, I think she has a point. There is a special energy between Fredy and me that makes me wonder if perhaps I were in a different mindset, we would be a good couple.

Fredy and the author, 2005

When thinking about doing this documentary project, the idea had crossed my mind that it would be amazing to go back to the jungle with Fredy and meet his family, to see what his tribal culture was really like. But I thought Fredy would not want to go, or that he would not know where to start looking for his family. Then, to my surprise, at the end of my first week back on San Cristóbal, Fredy showed me pictures from a trip he had made back to the jungle in the past few years, so going there now seemed like an actual possibility. I explained to Fredy how important such a trip would be for my project and offered to pay for his part of the travels. He considered for a couple of days, then told me all right. I was ecstatic—what an opportunity! Fredy gave me a guidebook done by a company in Madrid that included maps and information about the Ecuadorian Amazon. We went to the airport and I bought tickets for us to fly to Quito and spend just over a week on the mainland before I returned to the United States.

The interview excerpts in the following chapters were recorded in September of 2005 with Fredy and his friends and acquaintances on San Cristóbal Island, and later, with the exception of the interview with Victor, translated them from Spanish into English. During my visit at Fredy's cousin Fausto's in the jungle, I recorded two interviews with Fausto that were unfortunately lost due to a technical error with my minidisc recorder.

All of the secondary source research included in these chapters was done after my return from Ecuador, and, as you will note, the degree of discrepancy in the information from those two means varies greatly. My conversations with Fredy were not colored by the information I later learned, but neither did I have the information at my disposal to press Fredy to clarify some of his responses in light of "facts."

Can truth vary across cultures? Is truth more important than story, if the two can convey the same basic meaning? From my vantage point as someone torn between trust in the rational, scientific, Western intellectual way of understanding the world and a desire to rebel against that toward a simpler, purer, and less restrained way of existence, I believe that personal story and research are both valuable. My inclusion of both is perhaps reflective of my current position as a nomad searching for my ideal way of life, torn between a complex upbringing and longings for the simple.

IN SEARCH OF THE PRIMITIVE

> Savage: [noun] a member of a people regarded as primitive and uncivilized; a brutal or vicious person. Origin: Middle English: from Old French *sauvage* 'wild,' from Latin *silvaticus* 'of the woods,' from *silva* 'a wood.'
>
> Sophisticate: [verb] to cause (a person or their thoughts, attitudes, and expectations) to become less simple or straightforward through education or experience. Origin: late Middle English (as an adjective in the sense [adulterated,] as a verb in the sense [mix with a foreign substance]: from Medieval Latin *sophisticatus* 'tampered with.'[3]

In *The Savage: a history of misunderstanding*, Andrew Sinclair points out that "savage" did not always mean something ferocious; in its original meaning, the word was as innocent as the woods. Over years of use, the ferocious implication that is now carried by the word has been imposed on it. He explains that at the end of the Middle Ages, there was a trend to condemn foreign people as bestial. "To be human," he explains, "one had to be an urban man, far from the wild woods and the beings within them."[4] Yet, Sinclair argues that this Victorian belief in the superiority of civilization has been eroded. He describes a large increase in what he calls the

---

[3] New Oxford American Dictionary.
[4] Sinclair, *The Naked Savage*, 27.

"ambivalent self-consciousness of modern man."[5] In Medieval and Renaissance art, Sinclair observes, nakedness, a sign of savagery, was a mark of both innocence and evil. He writes that this duality extends to modern times, where there is a tendency to both glorify and denounce primitive people.[6]

Like the word "savage," the word "sophisticate" or "sophisticated," which is commonly used to mean highly developed, capable, and experienced, actually comes from a word with negative meanings. Over time, it seems like people's attitudes change with regard to which is better: the simple, natural, and uncorrupted, or the crafted, complicated, and advanced. Sometimes I think I am now part of a wave from the latter group who is gravitating back toward the former.

> ```
> Primitivism: [noun] a belief in the
> value of what is simple and
> unsophisticated, expressed as a
> philosophy of life or through art
> or literature.
> ```
>
> "...Primitivism became a medium of soul-searching and self-transformation in which the idea of merging has been key, especially for people who feel ill at ease or constrained in the West."[7]
> —Marianna Torgovnick, *Primitive Passions*

Primitivism is a philosophy of which Roger Sandall is sharply critical. In his book, *The Culture*

---

[5] Sinclair, *The Naked Savage*, 68.
[6] Sinclair, *The Naked Savage*, 144.
[7] Torgovnick, *Primitive Passions*, 13.

Cult: Designer Tribalism and Other Essays, Sandall describes a phenomenon that he calls "the Culture Cult," in which people view all cultures as equal and take a romantic view of simplicity and a sour view of modernity. He writes, "The romantic primitivism of the Culture Cult did not originate among tribal people themselves. Nor is it found among the poor. It is a Western sentimentalism fashionable among spoiled, white, discontented urbanites."[8] Sandall lists literacy and healthcare as two "undeniable benefits" of civilization, but complains that as a result of the "Culture Cult," the word "civilization" is hardly used anymore, because it indicates that the writer or speaker of the word considers the developed, Western cities, for instance, superior to more traditional, rural modes of existence. Of the latter, Sandall declares: "Most traditional cultures feature domestic repression, economic backwardness, endemic disease, religious fanaticism, and severe artistic constraints. If you want to live a full life and die in your bed, then civilization—not romantic ethnicity—deserves your thoughtful vote."[9]

    While I may be somewhat spoiled compared with most people in the world and could possibly have sentimental tendencies, I tend to agree more with other views on simplicity. In his book *A Handmade Life*, for instance, William S. Coperthwaite writes that simplicity "has long been recognized as a necessity by those aspiring to reach a higher plane of existence." From his home in rural Maine,

---

[8] Sandall, *The Culture Cult*, x.
[9] Sandall, *The Culture Cult*, ix.

Coperthwaite advocates and practices a life that involves as little excessiveness as possible; that is, a life that is close to the land, that is not wasteful of the earth's resources, and that generally shuns the American ideal that the collection of bigger and better stuff will lead to happiness.

When Fredy told me back in 2001 that he came from a cannibalistic tribe, my reaction was not one of fear or horror, but rather intrigue. The other *gringas* and I who hear Fredy's story of coming from a primitive jungle tribe are fascinated by his tale, not just because it is different from what we have experienced, but because through being with Fredy we feel that we are making a tie to some more essential part of ourselves and of human experience that modern life in the West makes difficult or impossible. As Marianna Torgovnick writes in *Primitive Passions*, "...the primitive is the sign and symbol of desires the West has sought to repress—desires for direct correspondences between bodies and things, direct correspondences between experience and language, direct correspondences between individual beings and the collective life force. It is the sign and symbol of desire for a full and sated sense of the universe."[10]

Part of my interest in getting Fredy's story was this sense that it was important in connecting me with the larger forces in the world and better understanding who I was as a living, breathing creature. I start my interviews with Fredy in what will become our normal interview location: Fredy's bed in

---

[10] Torgovnick, *Primitive Passions*, 8.

his small apartment. "What's your name?" I ask, laughing.

My original name is Shiguani,[11] which means green bird of the sun. There in the jungle, people are named after plants, rivers, the sun, things like that.

Andi, Fredy's current last name, morphed from the last part of his former name, Shiguani, means sun and is from Fredy's mother. He says that there is a green bird in the jungle that reflects sun like a mirror, and that is what he is named after.

Where exactly were you born?

In the Amazon region of Ecuador, in a national park called Yasuní. The park was formed by the Ecuadorian government about fifteen years ago.

And what was the name of your tribe?

The Huaorani.[12]

The Huaorani are known across Ecuador as the last Stone Age tribe in the Amazon.[13] Not only are they famous for being extremely primitive, they are also known for extreme violence, attacking and killing anyone who ventured into their 8,000-square-

---

[11] Pronounced "shee-HWA-nee." Fredy prefers this spelling with "Sh" to my suggested "X," but agrees that it was never a written name.
[12] pronounced "wow-RAH-nee," also spelled Waorani or Waodani.
[13] Rival, *Hijos del sol, padres del jaguar.*

mile territory, which was traditionally in the upper Amazon jungle in the provinces of Napo and Pastaza.[14]

Ecuadorians have long used the Quechua term *Auca*, which means savage or killer, to refer to the Huaorani. There is apparently a soccer team named after the tribe, similar to "Braves" as a name for a baseball team in the United States—as Ziegler-Otero observes, the Huaorani represent for Ecuadorians the "wild side of the national character."[15] Anthropologist Clayton Robarchek writes in his book, *Waorani: The Contexts of Violence and War*, "Although [the Waorani] possessed no firearms and in the last years of their isolation numbered fewer than 700, their fearsome reputation and viciously barbed 9-foot palmwood spears allowed them to maintain control over a vast territory, some 8,000 square miles of densely forested valleys, ridges, and swamps lying between the Napo and Curaray Rivers. With only those spears, they kept the modern world at bay until well into the second half of the twentieth century."[16]

Yasuní National Park was created in 1979 and is classified by UNESCO as a world biosphere reserve. In 1990, the Ecuadorian government gave 135,000 acres of the park to the Huaorani.[17]

When were you born?

[In the jungle] there's no register of how old a person is. I

---

[14] Smith, *Crisis Under the Canopy*.
[15] Ziegler-Otero, *Resistance in an Amazonian Community*, 26.
[16] Robarcheck, Waorani, 9.
[17] Smith, *Crisis Under the Canopy*, 11.

only suppose that I am 25, or 26, or 27.

What does your cédula[18] say?

That I am thirty. 1975.

Facts like dates are not Fredy's strong point. Fredy had told me that he was twenty-six last time I was on the Galápagos, four years previously, so I know I need to look further to get any precise answers about his age. Later on during our first day of interviews, I notice his *cédula* lying around his apartment and see that it actually says that he was born in 1974, which would make him thirty-one. I am also confused by the name the document lists for him: Humberto Fabian Shigua Andi. When I press him about these details, Fredy says that Shigua Andi is what the authorities turned Shiguani into, and that Fredy is a name he gave to himself about five years ago, before which he was known as Fabian. He doesn't seem to know or care about the Humberto part of his legal name or his official date of birth; he says he always just says he's thirty, that no one keeps track of birthdays in the jungle and he's never really tried to calculate. I feel a connection with Joe Kane, who tried to conduct a census of the Huaorani in the early nineties, when he writes in his book *Savages* of his difficulty in getting people's ages: "The only number that really meant anything was 'enough,' which you either had or had not."[19] Yet Kane also admits that even if precision were possible, "Simple

---

[18] Ecuadorian national identity card
[19] Smith, *Crisis Under the Canopy*, 36.

data would never explain the Huaorani. Such explanations as there were lay obliquely, if at all, amid snakes and hunger and mud and a forest so dense you rarely saw the sky."[20]

Observing Fredy's actions, it makes sense that "enough" was more meaningful in the jungle than precise numbers. On the Galápagos, Fredy seems always to have enough, although materially, with the exception of his expensive sunglasses, perhaps, he lives with very little. As we walk through the streets of Puerto Baquerizo Moreno, guys often shout in greeting to Fredy, "Billa*bong*!" with extra stress on the second syllable of his nickname. "Hey, what a champ," they seem to be saying. "You've managed to get with yet another *gringa*!"

> "The [Huaorani] over on the Catholic side are all savages. Pure savages. I can't think of any other word for people who kill their own kind....Of course, you can't help but like them. They're the most charming killers there ever was."
> —Rachel Saint, missionary[21]

Anthropologist James Yost has written that the Huaorani are the world's most violent culture, with more than sixty percent of adult deaths among the Huaorani over a span of five generations were caused by warfare.[22] Robarchek explains, "Their reputation for ferocity was, in fact, well founded....blood feuds

---

[20] Kane, *Savages*, 58.
[21] Kane, *Savages*, 87.
[22] Yost, "Twenty Years of Contact," 687.

and vendettas arising from past killings, from quarrels over marriage arrangements, and from accusations of sorcery were a way of life among the widely dispersed extended family bands."[23]

As Joe Kane, in his book *Savages* asks, however, who is more savage? We Westerners, who in modern warfare kill without wanting to, or the Huaorani, who kill with a "spiritual discipline"?[24]

Lino Tagliani, an Italian who spent four years among the Huaorani, says that war is a natural and essential part of the Huaorani way of life. "War is sacred because it has preserved their freedom up till now," he writes. "In fact, the Huaorani are warriors by birth and profession." Tagliani continues, "For a Huao warrior, the first duty is revenge of the received offense."[25]

Kane affirms this, writing that the Huaorani believe that all human deaths are caused by other humans and need to be avenged.[26] He notes, in fact, that there are very few old men in the tribe because so many of them have been killed.

What were your parents like?

Really twenty years ago, it was like wild life. We didn't need to worry about money, about having to go and work at a company....We lived just from hunting, fishing, and growing corn, yuca, and vegetables.

---

[23] Robarcheck, *Waorani*, 9.
[24] Kane, *Savages*, 75.
[25] Tagliani, *También el Sol Muere*, 44–45.
[26] Kane, *Savages*, 39.

Did you pass the time doing other things, too?

Yes, being with the family. There's always plenty to do. But not going to work to make money. What we did there was exchange. If you have corn, I have yuca. It's exchange. There wasn't any special form of money.

How did you spend your childhood?

In the jungle, in the rivers, swimming in the rivers....Life was truly wild. There wasn't even a ball to play with...you could only play with vines from the trees, more or less like Tarzan.

**Fredy demonstrating swinging from a vine,
Amazon region near Coca, 2005**

Did you live in a house, or what?

No, like small huts, made of palm trees, like the coconut palm, but specially constructed, by hand...and woven by hand too. Very pretty. It was like a kind of cabin.

Was there space to cook inside?

There there were no beds, but hammocks, always hammocks....

Fredy describes waking up in a hammock, next to the hammocks of his siblings and parents, arranged around the fire.

We didn't have steel pots either, like there are now....We would make pots out of mud, made by hand, and there was like a wax, that came from the trees, and we collected that and that gave it the final touch so it could stay hard and stand the fire....

Fredy's mother and oldest sister would already be up, preparing the typical drink and food source, the fermented *chicha de yuca,* from the potato-like yuca, or cassava, which Fredy describes as the "fountain of life," "like what beer is here in Galápagos." (Maybe for most dwellers. My Galápagos life never included beer.) Six brothers and six sisters, all from the same parents, and he's in the middle. "And do you know why there are so many children?" he asks me. "Because they didn't have television back there!"

From Fredy's descriptions of the jungle, it does sound like his former lifestyle could be easily idealized. As anthropologist Laura Rival, who has spent time living with and studying the Huaorani, writes:

> "Men, women and children spend a great part of their lives slowly exploring the forest. They hunt and gather, of course, but they also simply *walk*, observing with evident pleasure and interest animal movements, the progress of fruit maturation, or vegetation growth. When walking in this fashion, that is, when being in and *with* the forest, the body absorbing its smells, people never complain about getting tired or lost....I came to understand that the Huaorani territory is not definable from without as a well-demarcated space bounded by clear limits on all sides. It is, rather, a fluid and ever evolving network of paths used by people when 'walking in the forest.'"[27]

Not everything sounds ideal, however:

In general, people from the jungle are very machista. *The woman in the house, the men go out, and when the men return home, the food and everything else has to be ready...and if it isn't, there are problems. And surely they will fight....*

Sometimes the *chicha de yuca* can be a problem, too, Fredy says.

---

[27] Rival, *Trekking Through History*, xxix.

If you leave it to ferment for four or five days, it becomes very strong and the men get drunk and become very machista....They always want to order the women around. The women usually have more control with the chicha, but the men get drunk, and become aggressive.

What is valued most in women there? Beauty?

No, there women are valued most when they are hardworking, and very active, and like to do men's tasks sometimes, like hunt.

    Fredy says that in the jungle they hunted with bow and arrow, or with spears, which men could aim and strike right in the center of something twenty meters away, or with a blowgun, with darts tipped in poison such as snake venom. The women were almost always the ones to cook, Fredy says. When I ask him about a typical dish that they ate, he talks about one with a certain type of fish wrapped in leaves, but says seriously that they ate everything that moved, including monkeys, birds, snakes, fish, deer, wild pigs, and insects. Fredy gets a kick out of telling this to people on the Galápagos. "I eat everything that moves," he says, "So don't move." It seems to impress people.

    Fredy always seems to impress the foreign girls, especially, partly because he always seems to be happy, and knows how to spread his positive vibrations to others.

In a description of Huaorani lifestyle, Michael Seyfert, maker of the documentary film *Los Soberanos*, writes the following:

> "How they laugh, how they enjoy! With a complete sincerity in each movement, in each sentence and in each silence. One cannot help but be moved by the perfect integration that they seem to have attained between their minds, spirits and bodies, and at the same time with the divine energy of the universe. They are absolute sovereigns: free from doubts, free from restrictions and from internal chaos."[28]

While Seyfert writes this about life in the jungle, this is what I find, or idealize, about life in the Galápagos!

Seyfert is not the only person I find enamored with the Huaorani mode of existence. Missionary Elisabeth Elliot, who lived among the Huaorani in the late fifties, writes in her book, *The Savage, My Kinsman*, of the simplicity and yet fullness of Huaorani lives. In a chapter entitled, "The Best Things in Life are Free," she writes that despite the lack of stimuli in the jungle compared to in our modern cities, the Huaorani find plenty to do. Huaorani women spend a lot of time rolling string to make hammocks and fish nets, and Huaorani men are often busy sharpening spears or making poison darts. Elliot calls conversation "the commonest form of

---

[28] http://www.lossoberanos.com

entertainment" in the Huaorani lifestyle and says that the Huaorani will often laugh over a pot falling, show great glee and talk animatedly about a rooster fight, and spend a lot of time watching wildlife intently and teasing animals and children.[29]

Karl Dieter Gartelmann, writing about the Huaorani system of general agreement, of taking action based on unanimous decision, goes so far as to say, "…in the field of human behaviour within the society, the Indian seems to have evolved further than we have." Gartelmann notes that unlike the Huaorani, the Western world suffers from much conflict because of differing ideologies and socio-economic divides. "We are obliged to make use of a complicated system of laws, regulations and obligations to maintain order. And there were those "savages," apparently well-adjusted and living in the heart of an equally well-ordered society."[30]

Lino Tagliani, an Italian missionary from the Congregación de la Consolata who spent four years living with the Huaorani, during which time he became a self-described vagabond and dreamer, also seems hooked on the Huaorani way of life. He writes of Fredy's people:

> "They have so much to teach us! From them we have learned that the things that matter are very small: it is enough to be content with only the necessary, because the only things that exist in abundance are the sky, the land, and the jungle. To rediscover the

---

[29] Elliot, *The Savage, My Kinsman*, 127–131.
[30] Gartelmann, *El Mundo Perdido de los Aucas*, 23.

instinct of the senses, the equilibrium of the body....They have taught us above all that the mind and the heart existed before human science."[31]

I feel like I can relate Fredy to these descriptions of Huaorani life, however idealized they may be. This kind of "perfect integration," this balance of energy and body, action and reaction, is what I'd imagined made Fredy such a good dancer back in 2001. We continue our interview.

You told me four years ago that your tribe was descended from the Incas. Is that right?

[In the jungle] it is a mystery where your parents came from. Because they never wrote a book....You can't say, I come from Spain, and my mother was from Ireland...no, I have an ancestry purely from the jungle.[32]

Did you ever talk about the past?

No...my parents did not teach me about the history of the tribe, more about hunting, fishing, anacondas and crocodiles.[33] They would warn about not going to a certain lake, for instance, but not tell long stories. There were only practical stories....

---

[31] Tagliani, *También el Sol Muere*, 214.
[32] Adrian Warren of *BBC Wildlife Magazine* confirms that the Huaorani have "no history other than a tribal recollection that their ancestors came from "downriver; long ago." ("Waorani" 1984)
[33] perhaps the crocodiles Fredy speaks of are really caimans, as research indicates

Fredy admits that his parents never mentioned the word "Inca," that they in fact never mentioned their ancestors at all. He learned what he assumes now about his ancestry during a recent trip to Machu Picchu in Peru.

What language did you speak in the jungle?

Huaorani and Quechua, because we were near the border of the Cofanes, who spoke Quechua.

Could the different tribes communicate with one another?

A little bit, but not much. It's like French people knowing Italian, because they're close by.

Fredy tells me that he has now forgotten the Huaorani language, but remembers some Quechua. From all of his contacts with foreign tourists, he now actually speaks more English than Quechua. Yet, when he went back to visit his family, he says, he communicated with them in Quechua because it was easier. They speak Quechua now, apparently, as a result increased communication and exchange.

Like, I give you salt, you give me corn. I give you rice, you give me fish. The tribes talk to one another now....it's like free exchange. Because they now wear clothes, and they don't have a savage mentality now....now they have radio.

The younger generation of his tribe now is multilingual, speaking Huaorani, Quechua and Spanish, Fredy explains. The young people need to know Spanish, Fredy says, because the oil companies hire people from the jungle to help their workers get around safely amid dangerous spiders and small snakes, anacondas, and the quicksand in the swamp areas.

Laura Rival and Ziegler-Otero have noted that Huao Terero, the language of the Huaorani, is known by linguists as a language isolate, meaning it does not appear to be related to any other language. Like the origins of the Huaorani language, the origins of the Huaorani people remain mysterious: the only thing that is known is that the Huaorani existed in their current territory by the time of the rubber boom in the late nineteenth and early twentieth centuries.[34] According to Randy Smith, the Huaorani were victims of persecution during the rubber trade from 1875–1925 and were sold in slave markets in Iquitos and Manaus. They sought refuge deeper in the jungle and remained isolated until their contact with missionaries in the 1950s.[35]

How many people were in your tribe?

Now there are very few....Now we're in danger of extinction, like the Galápagos turtles on the islands here....Now the national park tells us that we are not allowed to leave the park. All the [Huaorani] who are in the park now are not allowed to leave and go to the city....

Why not?

---

[34] Ziegler-Otero, *Resistance in an Amazonian Community*, 25.
[35] Smith, *Crisis Under the Canopy*, 13.

Because you can't have a husband or wife who's not from the same tribe, because they don't want to lose the race.

The park wants to preserve the tribes?

Yes, and if they know that I am here they can deport me again....

In 1990, the Ecuadorian government granted the Huaorani a territory of 2,600 square miles, or about one third of the area of their traditional homeland.[36] The related contract specified that the Huaorani could not try to impede the extraction of oil or any other resource from their territory.

In 1993, Randy Smith conducted a census of all the Huaorani people. He counted 1,282 Huaorani in total, 647 male and 635 female, with twenty of these of mixed Quechua or Shuar ethnicity. Over fifty-seven percent of the population was under twenty, and just over a third of the Huaorani population was living in Toñampari, a community established inside a region called the Protectorate that was set up for the Huaorani by missionaries. Smith counted eighteen communities in total, with three in Yasuní National Park, ten in the Protectorate, two just outside the borders of the Protectorate, and three in the adjusted 1990 Huaorani territory.[37]

When I press Fredy later to tell me how many people were in his tribe, he says that maybe there

---

[36] Kane, *Savages*.
[37] Smith, *Crisis Under the Canopy*, 15.

were about fifty families in his community. I cannot get him to give me a clear picture of the setup of the tribe and its neighbors, though, because his information seems to change each time I ask. Fredy does tell me that something that distinguished the Huaorani from the surrounding tribes was a distended earlobe with a large hole in it, created by inserting larger and larger circular wooden plugs into the earlobe. I look at Fredy's ear, which seems normal to me. No, that stopped during my parents' generation, Fredy says. He goes on to explain that another tribe, the Patarojas, could also be easily distinguished because they painted their feet red.

The Patarojas are the only tribe in the Ecuadorian Amazon that are still not civilized.

And why aren't they civilized?

Because they don't want to become civilized. So the national park made another park for them, near the border. They live over there, and us here, near them. But now, you can't enter there, because they will kill you.

No one enters? Even the authorities?

No, no one. They are the only remaining savage tribe. They live without clothes....

And do you know people from that tribe?

I have seen them, but it's very difficult because they are inside the jungle...in the trees. And they have put up markers, like of heads, of the tribes they have fought and they've put up heads as a signal that if you pass through here, they will kill you.

Are they cannibals?

They kill to preserve their tribe.

And did your tribe have a similar culture to theirs?

Yes, similar. But we were more tranquil, whereas they were more aggressive because they're more savage. Because they have never seen a car; they've never seen anything....One time, white people[38] wanted to come in and conquer, but...no, the state of Ecuador said it's better if we make it so they live on their own.

And why did your tribe want to become civilized but theirs didn't?

They civilized us, not because we wanted to become civilized.

But you didn't resist like they did?

We did resist like they did. But sometimes, with the [oil] companies, they were very close to us, and the [Patarojas] farther away....So it was very difficult for the white people to pass through the two tribes....

Ziegler-Otero writes that Huaorani society is broken into *nanicabos*, or longhouse groups, which are

---

[38] Fredy uses the word *blancos*, or white people, to refer to both Latin Ecuadorians and whites from Europe and North America.

residential units of extended families.[39] He writes that the Huaorani have no formally recognized leaders, though he admits that shamans and older people are somewhat more influential.[40] Surprisingly to me, after hearing Fredy's story about his ascendance to be king of his tribe, much, in fact, has been written about egalitarianism within Huaorani culture. According to James Yost, for example, "Contrary to popular belief, the Waorani had no 'chiefs.'" Instead, Yost explains, they were mostly egalitarian with leadership designated only in certain situations.[41] Robarchek and Robarchek are even more vehement: "Waorani society is egalitarian in the extreme and every residence group is completely autonomous. Within these groups, there are no headmen and no formal councils....Even parents have little control over the actions of their children and cannot force them to do what they do not want to do."[42] Karl Dieter Gartelmann, however, mentions the chief or *cacique*[43] in his book on the Huaorani and says that the life of the *cacique* was intimately connected to the life of the Harpy eagle. He writes, "Each individual group lives under the far-from-strict leadership of a chief. This position usually falls to the one who distinguishes himself in hunting, and in war expeditions. He is a leader, but in point of fact has very little real authority."[44]

---

[39] Ziegler-Otero, *Resistance in an Amazonian Community*, 37.
[40] Ziegler-Otero, *Resistance in an Amazonian Community*, 43.
[41] Yost, "Twenty Years of Contact," 692.
[42] Robarchek and Robarchek, "Cultures of War and Peace," 102.
[43] pronounced "kah-SEE-kay"
[44] Gartelmann, *El Mundo Perdido de los Aucas*, 120–124.

It seems that despite the high level of violence within Huaorani society, then, Huaorani culture also places strong value on harmony. According to Kane, the highest title a Huao can attain is *ahuene*, which means "the one who makes peace."[45]

Fredy and I talk about the role of the *cacique*, or chief.

What is the role of the cacique *in the tribe?*

The role of the cacique is to organize the people, like when there is a ceremony…to call a meeting about when they are going to celebrate the…moon, or a wedding, or something like that. He leads so that he can give messages to other people.

What characteristics does a cacique *need to be a good one?*

He has to be very capable, have a lot of knowledge about everything, and know the other tribes that the tribe has been at war with, and know some shamanism to cure people.

Fredy explains that being a good *cacique* doesn't have to do with being the strongest warrior, but rather being good at working with people.

Was your father a good cacique?

---

[45] Kane, *Savages*, 137.

Yes, and a good hunter...and knowledgeable about medicinal plants. He knew which plant to use if you had a headache, or nausea.

What was he like as a person?

He was very charitable with everyone...he never judged other people; he only supported them. And sometimes, when there were problems in a family, he would go and resolve them.

Were you stronger or weaker than others in the jungle?

In the jungle, no one is better than anyone. Everyone has his talent, his gift.

What was your gift? Why did they choose you to be the next cacique *rather than one of your brothers?*

I was brighter...I was more creative, more active...They always looked for the person whose mind was a bit more open, a person who could become a shaman. I knew how to do a few things with leaves, with fire, to cure people.

It seems like Fredy does have special shamanic powers. He certainly has physical powers. He told me that he was going to come over at around eight one evening, so we could watch a movie, but he came around six and found me starting to prepare dinner with *zapallo*, a pumpkin-like squash, pasta and onion. Thinking that he could do a better job, he proceeded to cut the *zapallo* and onion for me, and despite my cooking experience he was in fact a lot more skilled with the knife. Then, when the water for the pasta was boiling and there weren't any potholders, I thought of Fredy and his tough hands and asked him to do it. Sure enough, he said the metal handles weren't even hot to the touch for him. Fredy took the knife he was using, and while I had my eyes turned, quickly went zap, zap with it along the under edge of the tile countertop. His movement was so quick, so concentrated with energy, that I asked him to do it again so I could watch. It sharpens the knife, he said.

I was very agile in doing everything....They would tell me to do things, or collect things, like eggs from birds or turtles. And I was very fast, I always knew where I could find the eggs. I had the instinct that enabled me to find them. And here, sometimes, I use that same instinct, to know what is going to happen later on. But in a different system.

Fredy often says that he knows when things are going to happen, that he has a certain sixth sense. When we rented a DVD, for instance, for the DVD player attached to the TV in my room, Fredy said on the walk back that oh no, the DVD player may not work. And sure enough, we could not get the DVD player to work. (I finally did, by asserting that "yellow goes with yellow" and really impressed Fredy with this technological know-how.) When he is watching movies, too, he apparently knows most times what is going to happen. Fredy says that this sense also told him, back four years ago, that I would return to the Galápagos one day, and that he would see me again. He says this sense he has relates to his shaman-like qualities, which were possibly passed down to him by his father.

Fredy says that his father was a shaman as well as *cacique*, and this is confusing to me, as I've heard Fredy use both terms to describe what he was going to become.

Are cacique *and shaman the same thing?*

Shamans are leaders who have special knowledge of how to use plants to cure people. There are usually two or three in each community. The cacique *is the leader of the tribe. The shaman cures people, but also has a high status so that he could be* cacique.

Fredy explains that the shamans traditionally always wore a crown of feathers and a necklace of tiger teeth or other animal bones carved as teeth.

How do people become shamans?

It's a gift…something that grows within you, that inside of you there is something that makes you able to do more than others. It's not difficult for you to do things, understand? You have a gift that, for instance, I touch you, and your arm falls asleep. It could be like that. Or, I tell you, sleep, and you sleep. You have a gift that you can cure people.

The shamans take ayahuasca,[46] *too, and through this they can see who is capable of being a shaman. They chose me to do like they did. They said, "I saw that you can."*

---

[46] pronounced "ah-ya-WAH-ska"—a hallucinogenic drug prepared from an Amazonian vine

Fredy explains that there are good shamans and bad shamans. The bad ones communicate with the evil gods and do things like send a bird to your house, that sits right in front of you, and you catch it because it is pretty. Then the bird leaves and after a half hour or an hour, you start to convulse and spit foam.

Why do they do this?

They are jealous of something; they are bad people.

He says it's never happened to him personally, but to his family, yes.

Fredy talks about the belief in the jungle that if you fall ill, it is because someone has hurt you. An egg is sometimes used to see if someone has harmed you: the shaman passes the egg over your body, and then cracks it into a glass of water. If someone has hurt you, white things fall down through the water. But if not, the water remains all clear.

I am waiting to learn more about Fredy's cannibalistic past, but am slightly embarrassed to ask about it directly. In our third interview, I broach the subject and pressure him to tell me about the cannibalism in his tribe that he mentioned to me in 2001.

Yes, a long time ago, before the civilization of the tribe, there were intertribal wars in which we would take prisoners and kill them with spears.

Do you remember this?

Of course.

Were you there watching?

Yes, I was a small child. And the children never go to war; they stay hidden, like in caves....

And what do you remember specifically about when your tribe ate someone?

It was like...it was fine for them, but for me, I tried it, but...wild animal meat tasted better.

Was there some special ceremony?

Yes, of course. And everyone had to take parts of the human body.

Was there only a single body?

Yes. And I ate the lips, which are delicious. That is why I like to kiss a lot.

Was cannibalism something normal, that you did?

We did it in wars, in triumph, after we had won. Only when you won in a war, not in normal life.

Who was your tribe fighting with?

With another tribe. We were surrounded by other tribes, and we didn't know which it was.

You didn't know who you were fighting?

No, not until you saw the person....Now the white people have given names to the tribes, like Cofanes, or Achuar, to write their books. But before, they didn't have names.

There weren't names for the tribes before?

No. Just the white people put those names in their books.

How was it, then?

There were tribes here, tribes there, but without names. One community here, another there, nothing else. Now, yes, they have names. **They have a name for everyone.**

The word "Huaorani" means "the true people" or "human beings." According to anthropologists like Robarchek and Rival, the Huaorani call all outsiders *cowode*,[47] which means foreign cannibals. So on the one hand, the Huaorani have long been seen by outsiders as cannibals. As Clayton Robarchek describes, "...the savage *Aucas*, naked cannibals who kill with spears and sorcery and devour the flesh of their victims."[48] On the other hand, though, it seems that the Huaorani themselves used the notion of cannibalism to distinguish themselves as the true people, and all other people as the more savage, subhuman flesh eaters. As Priscilla Walton writes, Europeans have also used the idea of cannibalism to

---

[47] also spelled *cohuori, kowudî*
[48] Robarchek, *Waorani*, 9.

distinguish between savagery and civility. For the purposes of colonialism, she explains, such "'uncivilized practices'...serve as justification for [the savages'] eradication or subordination."[49]

In his 1979 book *The Man-Eating Myth*, Jonathan Arens questions reports of cannibalism among primitive people and argues that the idea of cannibalism has more to do with Western prejudice than with truth. Whether completely based on prejudice or not, it seems clear that both the Huaorani and Europeans have used the notion of cannibalism to mean savage, dangerous foreigners. But perhaps accusations of cannibalism are worth their weight more in shock value than in truth.

For my own purposes, trying to find mention of cannibalism among the Huorani, my hands came up empty. Blanco Villalta, for instance, in his 1970 book on cannibal rites in the Americas, describes cannibalistic traditions observed in Brazil, for example, among the Tupinambaes, the Tupiguaraníes, and the Guaraníes, and in North America, among the Algonquin, Athapascos, and Aztecs, but he does not share any information about cannibalism in the region of Ecuador. In my research on the Huaorani, I did not find any reports of cannibalism or even a mention of it except by Robarchek, who writes of Huaorani accounts of cannibalism by outsiders to their tribe. "Although allegations of cannibalism are notoriously unreliable," he writes, "some *kowudi*[50] may, in fact, have eaten

---

[49] Walton, Our Cannibals, Ourselves, 17.
[50] variation of Huaorani word for foreign cannibals

human flesh."[51] Related to cannibalism, it seems that in Huaorani folklore itself, there is a story that the Huaorani ended up in their present location because their numbers were dwindling by being eaten by cannibals, so they had to flee farther and farther upriver.[52] It seems to me that this would indicate that the Huaorani themselves were not cannibals, because in the folktale they distinguish their people from others who were eating human flesh.

During my interviews with Fredy, I didn't press him hard as to whether his tribe was really cannibalistic or not; that aspect of his past, one of the first he had shared with me, I just assumed to be true. Fredy's description of the custom of shrunken heads was one part of his story that fit in well with the idea of cannibalism. He explains that there were strict limits between tribes in the jungle, and that these territorial boundaries were marked by shrunken heads of enemies or of whoever dared to trespass on their territory. To shrink the heads, Fredy says, there are big pots full of medicinal plants that make everything shrink.

I saw this one time. The heads come out dry…all intact, just in miniature. With hair, and bones…it's the heat of the vapor that does it, the heat of the plants, and the chemicals in the plants, make the head smaller. They would put the shrunken heads in the meeting houses, hanging.

---

[51] Robarchek, *Waorani*, 97.
[52] Robarchek, *Waorani*, 90.

Why didn't the heads rot? I ask. Fredy explains that the heads were completely dry and therefore kept for a long time.

The Ladder of Civilization

Edward Burnett Tylor in his 1881 book *Anthropology: An Introduction to the Study of Man and Civilization*, presents three stages of mankind: the savage, in which people subsist on wild plants and animals, the barbaric, in which they engage in farming and herding, and the civilized. The civilized stage began only with writing, according to Tylor, because writing bound together "the past and the future in an unbroken chain of intellectual and moral progress."[53]

Andrew Sinclair explains that the written word is a very important dividing line, one which leads to land being taken away from "savages." He writes:

> "In a mutable and everyday world, the stability of the written word, its power to record and prove the past, became a weapon in the minds of churches and civilized men. They believed that the word itself might be real, that what was visualized and inscribed was true....Yet for the primitive man, the two great realities other than himself were the realities of the world of the senses and of his society. For him, thought was only one mechanism for adjusting and controlling conflicts between the individual and his fellow man and

---

[53] Tylor, *Anthropology*, 24.

nature itself. Intuition and feeling and dream and totem were equally important in reconciling a person with his place in life."[54]

In writing this book, I am using one of the most fundamental pillars of civilization—writing. I was raised to be a reader, a thinker in this way of writing, and so I write, even though it may go against the simplicity of life I am seeking.

Fredy has a different relationship to writing. How did you learn to write? I asked him back in 2001. The answer was not clear, but I saw that he was able to type, if slowly and with numerous spelling errors, e-mails to his girlfriends and surfing buddies once they returned to Switzerland, Germany or the United States.

• • •

Thinking of my own country-jumping tendencies, I wonder whether the Huaorani, in contrast, were always fixed in one spot. Laura Rival writes that they were more foragers than gardeners, cultivating yuca, maize and plantain only sporadically.[55] I'm not sure if this meant that before being contacted they had permanent homes or not.

In the jungle, did your family or tribe stay in one place, or move around?

---

[54] Sinclair, *The Savage*, 19.
[55] Rival, *Trekking Through History*, 19.

As the oil companies entered, we kept going farther and farther into the jungle. Because twenty years ago, our community wasn't civilized, you know.

What do you mean, "civilized"?

We were on our own. We didn't know what a car was, or a plane, we only lived from hunting and fishing, and that's all. We were all in one place, and didn't know if there was a car, understand? [Our tribe] was virgin.

But, later?

Later, the oil companies, and the Catholic priests,[56] wanted to come in and civilize our tribe. About twenty or twenty-five years ago, there were a few priests who wanted to enter....they flew overhead and threw chocolates down from the air....They did this four or five times, and they thought that we were already civilized. Until one time, they entered into our community, and our families killed them. There were about two monks, a priest, and a pilot. We killed them because we wanted to be on our own, understand?....There was a big news report about that, about what happened.

    The Summer Institute of Linguistics is a worldwide evangelical network, headquartered in Texas, whose goal is to translate the Bible into indigenous tongues. It describes itself as "a faith-based organization that studies, documents, and assists in developing the world's lesser-known languages." In September of 1955, Protestant missionaries from the Summer Institute of Linguistics

---

[56] Perhaps Fredy means Protestant missionaries.

(SIL) and the Missionary Aviation Fellowship (MAF) began "Operation Auca," in which they attempted to contact a group of Huaorani near the Curaray River.[57] A *LIFE Magazine* article from January 1956 begins: "In the jungles of eastern Ecuador lives a tribe of Stone Age Indians called Aucas, little known even to anthropologists and until less than a month ago never photographed in their native surroundings." The article recounts the spearing of five missionaries by a group of Huaorani and refers to the killing as "martyrdom" on the part of the missionaries.[58]

From SIL missionary Nathaniel Saint's diary, October 2, 1955:

> "Last night Ed McCully, Jim Elliot, Johnny Keenan and I were on the living room floor on elbows and knees poring over a map of the eastern jungles of Ecuador. We had just decided that it was the Lord's time to try to contact the savage Auca tribe...."[59]

The article in *LIFE* describes how, over thirteen gift visits, Saint and his friends dropped ten machetes, eight kettles, six shirts, three pairs of pants, and lots of colored buttons and trinkets to the Huaorani.[60] The North American missionaries were then speared to death.

---

[57] Smith, *Crisis Under the Canopy*, 13.
[58] "Go Ye and Preach the Gospel," 10–12.
[59] "Go Ye and Preach the Gospel," 10–12.
[60] ibid.

Do you remember this?

Yes, of course.

What do you remember about it?

How the accident happened and what happened with them. There's a big river called Curaray River, where they landed, in a small plane outfitted to land in a river...Our community saw something really strange, like, wow, what is this, you know? And then we sank the plane.

Your tribe?

Yes, we sank it.

With what, stones?

Yes, we made holes, and then, down it went.

And then, you took out the bodies?

Yes, then...it's a really long story...the military came into the community, because they'd heard that a plane had tried to land there, but they didn't find anything, not the plane, or the pilot, or the monks, nothing. They came in, with guns...and we had never seen a gun, you know.

And what happened?

They found the bodies, but with the stab wounds we'd made, with lances.

But you didn't eat the bodies?

Almost. [He smiles.] We almost ate them, but then we decided not to.

What happened when the military came?

Those of us that were there, we fled into the jungle, to escape.

And they didn't catch you?

No, because we were very fast in the jungle, and without shoes. You can run even faster that way.

In the late sixties and seventies, missionary Rachel Saint, older sister of Nate Saint, who was one of the missionaries speared in the 1956 incident, and others from the Summer Institute of Linguistics arranged with the Ecuadorian government and the Texan oil company Texaco to lure most of the Huaorani into a small area called the "Protectorate" on the far western edge of the traditional Huaorani territory. Joe Kane believes that this move helped Texaco blaze the road known as the Vía Auca, and aided in further opening Huaorani territory to oil development and colonization.[61]

Kane says of Rachel Saint, who stayed and continued her missionary work among the Huaorani after the spearing of her brother, "She applied herself with a holy vengeance." "Within a few years," Kane writes, "through sheer stubbornness, the intimidating magic of airplanes and bullhorns, and the seductive

---

[61] Kane, *Savages*, 27.

luxury of salt, white rice, and aluminum pots, she'd managed to establish a Christian benchhead inside the Huaorani territory...."[62]

They threw down lots of chocolates, and caramels...and some of us liked it, but for others, it gave them a stomachache.

Did you think of the chocolates as a type of gift?

Yes, like a gift. But we never thought that it was going to be a system to civilize us. And later, they threw down clothing.

And did you know what to do with it?

No, we'd never seen it before. But, later, we thought it was great because we weren't cold anymore.

And after a time [of throwing down these gifts], [the missionaries] wanted to land, and enter our community. And that was their mistake. They thought that we were already civilized. With the chocolates, and the other things that they had thrown down, they thought that we were already tamed into wanting more of their things. And that was not true. Because we were savage!

The missionaries thought that we wouldn't hurt them because they were religious, but how are we going to know who is a priest, or if they are people of God? For us, they were just intruders....

---

[62] Kane, *Savages*, 20.

The documentary film *Beyond the Gates of Splendor* and the popular film *End of the Spear* that followed it both portray the 1956 spearing incident, mostly from the perspective of the missionaries and their families. Both films depict the Huaorani motivation for spearing the missionaries as stemming from a misunderstanding among members of their tribe, rather than a true desire to reject the advances of the missionaries and their encroachment into the Huaorani's isolated way of life.

They rescued the bodies that we'd killed with spears, and we fled. Afterwards, they caught one of us and civilized him. They taught him Spanish, so that he could translate. He came back to the jungle alone and told us about the different world outside. He came back to tell us that the people outside were good, because there were lots of things to see....and he went back and forth, giving us the information that he learned there, and bringing medicines...he was like an interpreter.

Who might this interpreter that Fredy mentions be? According to Randy Smith, Dayuma is the name of a Huaorani woman who helped Rachel Saint make contact with Huaorani groups and lead them to the Protectorate. Man writes that Dayuma fled from her tribe as a child and became the first Huaorani link to the outside world, while Kane describes how Rachel Saint presented Dayuma to the outside world as the leader of the Huaorani, when that was actually not at all the case. In 1973, Anthropologist James Yost wrote that Saint was trying to turn Huaorani culture into a matriarchy, with

Dayuma as its queen.[63]

Later, the priests[64] came, but guided by this person, so that the tribe wouldn't harm them.

Was this interpreter a member of your family?

A cousin, yes. And little by little, he became a teacher, to teach us that we were in a jungle and that there wasn't life here. Because [the outsiders] gave him some psychology...they taught him what to tell our tribe. He said that they could work for the oil company, and get more clothing, and more medicine, for times when the plant medicine was not enough.

Kane describes Toñampare, Rachel Saint's village in the Huaorani Protectorate area, as a collection of tin-roofed shacks with a radio constantly spewing out God stories and a toilet that was never used. Kane feels that Rachel Saint's remaking of Huaorani culture has definitely been bad for the Huaorani: he lists poor health, a scarcity of animals, and increased dependency as the ills that she has introduced, explaining that the Huaorani living in the Protectorate are now "wage slaves" to a culture that has considered them to be like animals.[65]

Moi Enomenga, who has become kind of a spokesman for the Huaorani, wrote in a letter to the U.S. president that was brought to Washington by the Sierra Club Legal Defense Fund, "We live with the

---

[63] Kane, *Savages*, 86.
[64] Again, perhaps Fredy means Protestant missionaries.
[65] Kane, *Savages*, 88.

spirit of the jaguar. We do not want to be civilized by your missionaries or killed by your oil companies. Must the jaguar die so that you can have more pollution and television?"[66]

Daphne Eviatar also quotes Moi Enomenga: "In the beginning, we accepted whatever the oil company offered," says Moi. "But after a while, we realized we didn't get any benefit. The gifts don't last. We can have everything—an airplane, a helicopter—but we can't maintain it." "Indeed," Eviatar writes, "it's the Huaoranis' growing dependence on the companies and their increased alienation from the rainforest that's steadily destroying their way of life."[67]

Moi's father, Ñame, rebelling against evangelical missionary influence, apparently established a community called Quehueire Ono at the northwest corner of the government-granted Huaorani territory. Kane says that there, in contrast to in the rest of the Protectorate, you can now find the "good life."[68] Kane reports that there is a synthesis of modern and traditional tools in Quehueire Ono that gives its inhabitants access to *abundancia*.[69] Literacy, in letting the Huaorani write threatening letters, for instance, gives the tribe access to tools, food, radios, boots, and airplanes.[70]

...

---

[66] Kane, *Savages*, 4.
[67] Eviatar, "The High Cost of Oil."
[68] Joe Kane, *Savages*, 136.
[69] abundance
[70] Kane, *Savages*, 137.

So that was the psychology that they gave [our tribe]. That it was going to be a change...we thought that we were going to have everything. Great! We never thought that later, we would have to work, to earn money, and buy. We thought that, wow! We are going to have everything. Understand? We thought that we were going to have everything, without having to work.

So it was disappointing for you, then?

Of course. But it was already too late to say, you know, we're not going to do this, because the psychology was already with us, guiding us to see more and go further ahead.

Why didn't you see the change as something negative from the start?

I don't know...it's like if you see something new, like a plane, or a hat, you want it and you want to see what more there is.

• • •

Kane describes the recent development of the Huaorani as a "leap from Stone Age to Petroleum Age."[71] He notes that the body of an adult Huao during the time he was conducting his census typically had several major scars, from staph infection, shotgun or outboard motor accidents, falls, and animal and snakebites. "Still," he writes, "...life

---

[71] Kane, *Savages*, 20.

among the Cononaco[72] was superior to life in the Protectorate, which was crowded and sedentary, and it was infinitely better than life along the Vía Auca—a life of, at best, canned tuna and Coca-Cola."[73]

•••

Your cousin, the interpreter, wasn't viewed as a traitor?

No, because he gave good things: he spoke of how incredible it was here....like if I left Galápagos and went to the jungle and told them how incredible it was here, and how much there is to do...that you can change your life, you can be somebody, you can study....this is what I told my brother. Come with me, and you can surf, and, I don't know, look for foreign girls. Easy!

And what did your brother say?

He said, yes, sure! Bring me with you. And I said yes, but now I don't have money. When I have money, I will bring you. And he does want to come. Everyone wants to come. Imagine!

•••

The details of Fredy's story of his tribe's first contact with missionaries seem to match up fairly well with the widely publicized spearing that occurred in 1956. However, given Fredy's age, he

---

[72] a group of Huaorani not living in the established Protectorate area
[73] Kane, *Savages*, 35.

clearly could not have even been born in 1956. So, the question remains: did Fredy pull from group memory about the arrival of the missionaries, and make up the part about his being present for effect? Could the style of life Fredy describes be real, even if his facts are not? Or, was he referring to an event that actually did happen during his lifetime?

Apparently, a different spearing of missionaries did occur during the early eighties by a group of Huaorani known as the Tagaeri, when Fredy would have been around ten:

> In 1985, the Catholic Misión Capuchina wrote up the "Plan de Amistad Tagaeri," a document signed by representatives of the oil company CPE (now Petroecuador) and the Catholic missionaries, whose purpose was to contact and befriend the Tagaeri. The groups conducted aerial search flights and dropped gifts between November of 1985 and April of 1996 to locate the Tagaeri. On July 21, 1987, Monseñor Labaca and Sister Inés Arango were dropped off by helicopter at a Tagaeri village on the shore of the Tiguino River, and were found the next day speared to death, the village abandoned.[74]

---

[74] Smith, *Crisis Under the Canopy*, 105–107.

Leaving the Tribe

Fredy's hands are large and thick. His fingers are much longer than mine, even though I am a few inches taller and have relatively big hands. His feet, too. They are big for his small body, but they seem to make sense that way. His hands and feet were everything to him in the jungle.

Fredy's hands are always warm and give amazing massages. He presses, moving in a downward scrubbing motion, and draws the blood back along my veins. After his touch, the life liquid flows more vigorously than before. He makes me moan with how good the massage is, and I am not one who easily shows appreciation. Somehow, though, Fredy can never stop at the massage. He kneads and presses down around my sides, lifting back my shirt, then down and underneath to massage my breasts. It feels really good. But he wants to go further, and this annoys me. I want to stay in that safe, cared for place, and he crosses my line into invasion. I don't think Fredy means to offend me, though. For him, sex is just a natural extension of physicality, not anything to be saved for the ideal emotional and intellectual connection.

...

With regard to sex and other aspects of life, John Man has noted a general lack of competitiveness among the Huaorani. For instance, when Man tried to organize a spear or stone-throwing competition, or taught the Huaorani how to play soccer, they did not pick up on the competitive spirit and the game became more of a farce. Relatedly, "Western concepts of love and marriage," Man writes, "founded on a system of jealously guarded monogamy, have no meaning to the Waorani and sex is not endowed with deep significance." Marriage, Man says, is a working partnership more than a love match, and multiple spouses are rarely jealous. A husband, according to Man, is free to have sex with his wife's sister, and a wife similarly free to do so with her husband's brother, "especially if he is a bachelor or has come a long way to visit."[75]

...

Perhaps this lack of competitiveness is related to a more laid-back attitude about things in general. Toward the end of my second week back on the Galápagos, I came to Fredy's room in the morning as usual, feeling like we had a lot of material we needed to cover. When I arrived, though, Fredy wanted to relax, and keep relaxing. We would interview later, he said. I didn't believe him and told him I didn't feel like relaxing. Upset, he accused, "You're like a robot." My liking to stick to a schedule was foreign to him.

In fact, there are lots of ways in which Fredy says I differ from other people, even *gringos*, he knows. For instance, he tells me and others that I'm the only one who can't seem to understand him when he talks in English; that's why we talk in Spanish. His English, even more so than his Spanish, seems to be

---

[75] Man, *Jungle Nomads of Ecuador*, 126.

specialized in conversational phrases for small talk with tourists—I want to discuss serious things with him, so I feel Spanish gives us a fuller chance to do this—plus his English really bothers me, surfer and bar talk, stutter, etc. Not being a native Spanish speaker, these things in Spanish don't bother me as much.

In terms of other differences, Fredy says, well, he's never been with someone who doesn't drink or smoke, and that normally he would be out *tomando* with his amigos during the day or night. Well, why aren't you out doing that now? I ask. I don't think you'd like that too much, he says, looking at me pointedly. Would you? Considering, I tell him, well, I am here to document your life, so in that sense I want you to do what you normally do. But right, I would not like it if I showed up at your apartment to interview you and you were drunk.

We move on with the morning's interview, and I ask Fredy to tell me about how he came from the jungle to the Galápagos.

When Huaorani boys reach the age of fifteen, Fredy explains, they are given a drug that allows them to see their future. The shaman, who is a sort of witch, or wise man, who knows how to use plants to cure people, cuts a plant called *ayahuasca*, which means *vena del diablo*, or devil's vein, into pieces and cooks it for seven or eight hours in a large quantity of water. Afterward, there remains only a small bit of liquid, which is an extremely powerful drug that causes a person to see his future. Before taking this drug, Fredy explains, you do not eat for two days in order to cleanse your body and spirit.

When I took [the ayahuasca*], it was like I was dreaming in another dimension. I saw that in time, I was not going to remain in the jungle....I saw that I was going to leave for a larger civilization, where there were many buildings, and cars...It was like, wow, well, how? You know? I had never seen these things before....I told [the shaman] what I saw in my dream and he said that you have to do what it tells you....I told everyone that I had to leave, and they thought that I was crazy, because I told them stories about what I'd seen in my dream.*

What type of stories?

That I was in a place with cars, buildings, strange people, traveling in an airplane, things like that—imagine!

Normally, people...

Normally they don't see that, they see other things from [the jungle]. I don't know what happened with me!

Fredy says he also saw in his dream a possible future of being *cacique* and of having many wives and children, but he was drawn to the mystery of the unfamiliar path. After this dream, Fredy felt his instinct tugging him, telling him that he had to leave his tribe, for it was no longer his life there. He wanted to know why he had seen the powerful vision he had—a vision that, according to Fredy, he did not only see, he also actually lived.

I am renewing my steps. What I saw [in that dream], I already did. This is only a recollection…all the things that I'm doing now, I've already done.

I don't understand. You're saying that you've already lived the life you're living now?

Yes, I've already lived it. Because I've seen all of this in my dream. Everything I do, I already know where I need to go after a while.

You know where you have to go? Where?

My dream was that I am not going to live here. I need to go farther still.

Here in the Galápagos?

Yes, here, I've already arrived here. In my dream I saw that I live on an island. And when I was in the civilization, I asked, where can I find an island? Galápagos. And how do I get to Galápagos? By plane. Ah, yes, by plane. Now I remember, I dreamed that I flew on an airplane. So I did it; I bought my ticket and came by plane. All of this was like sections…of a movie that I was watching. And in my dream I saw that I was going to have as a wife a tall, blond girl, but I haven't found her yet.

Fredy flashes me a conspiratorial smile, and puts his head on my lap. After a while of my prodding, we continue.

I've already seen that I have two sons.

Oh, really? So you're going to have two sons, then?

Yes, I always said that; I've always told people that I have two sons in my head. I don't know; I still have to look for the tall, blond girl.

And you know that you're not going to live here in Galápagos?

No, I will live in another region. But for now I'm still here.

• • •

Kane's description of the Huaorani Moi Enomenga reminds me of Fredy. He says that Moi is "naturally charming, with a poet's talent for interpreting life in ways that applied universally." "Moi has an ability to communicate with people that goes beyond the boundaries of language," Kane writes, and notes that a young tourist admirer remarked that Moi had a certain purity, that he seemed to "speak directly from his heart."[76]

• • •

What finally pushed you to go? Was there a particular night when you decided to leave?

Yes, one night I decided to go because my body was telling me to do that, to leave. It was an impulse, coming from inside of me.

Did you bring anything with you?

---

[76] Kane, *Savages*, 203, 222–223.

Yes, some bananas, and yuca, and fish, for the trip.

How did you know where to go?

I followed the river, because I had heard that farther down the river there was some machinery or something. So I went in that direction and listened for thunder sounds, that they were making with the dynamite....and soon I saw smoke, because I climbed high up in the trees, to see, trees that were some thirty meters high....

Did you leave your community at night?

No, in the daytime. At night, [to avoid being prey for snakes or other animals], I had to sleep up in a tree. I tied myself to a branch so I wouldn't fall.

Did you say goodbye to your family before you left?

Yes, I told them that I had to go because I had had that dream....and as I already had use of reason they said, fine then, you have to go.

What do you mean, you had use of reason?

I knew what I was doing. I...had to complete a mission.

Your family didn't try to get you to stay?

Yes, they did, but I said no, I have to go. And...they held a small ceremony, with drums...

As a farewell for you?

Yes, and the women danced around the fire.

Why?

As a farewell for the son of the cacique. *The son of the king. And then, I woke up at six in the morning, and I had to go.*

Were you going to marry someone at that point?

Yes, they had already found a bride for me. And I knew that I was to marry her the following day.

The day that you left your tribe, you were supposed to get married?

Yes, and I said, no, I have to go now. Because if I get married, that's it. There, when you marry someone, you respect the woman. She is not allowed to sleep with another man....It's like a law, that if a woman marries someone, and he goes away or dies, she is not allowed to have children.

Fredy talks about the sacredness of marriage in the jungle, but the values in his current lifestyle seem a lot different with regard to fidelity. I let the issue go for the time being, however, and he continues his story of coming to the Galápagos.

From the jungle, I followed the rivers, to where the oil companies were working. And there, I was still a bit savage. But with an instinct to move forward, to see things.

Fredy looked for the oil workers because he figured that, since they came from the outside, they would be able to help him leave the jungle. He worked with them for about two years, washing dishes and doing other odd jobs.

How did you communicate with them?

It was truly difficult. Very difficult. Because I knew my language, and they spoke in a totally different one.

Yet, via gestures, pointing, and the company workers telling him the words for things, Fredy learned to communicate in basic Spanish in about three months, he says. Later, they gave him magazines to look at, and he saw pictures of cars and other things from the modern world. Fredy wanted to see those things!

Little by little, Fredy recounts, he saved up money. The oil workers earned about fifty sucres per day, while he earned five, but still, in time it added up. (Five sucres was about three dollars, he says.) When one of the oil workers went home to a small Amazonian city called Tena for vacation, he asked Fredy if he would like to come along and Fredy was more than happy to go. They left the jungle in a dump truck....

And wow, we went to the city, and I was like this, [shakes] trembling, afraid, you know, because I'd never seen so many cars, and I was with long hair, you know? The company had given me work clothes and boots....

Fredy spent three or four years in Tena, staying with the family of that oil worker. The family had its origins in the Quechua tribe, and spoke Quechua as well as Spanish. Fredy became like a son to them, helping in the house and on their small farm, harvesting to dry and sell banana, coffee and cocoa.

I adapted very easily....

There in Tena he got documents with his new name, Humberto Fabian Shigua Andi, and he attended school with the two other children in the family, up to the fourth grade.

I hear what Fredy is saying, but my mind is still on the jungle, and on the idea of killing people and then eating them, an idea so far from my own experience. Trying to get at the cannibal issue again, I ask Fredy whether he himself ever went to war.

That depends on what war. I was in the war in 1992, over the border with Peru....

Fredy says that he and others who knew how to survive in the jungle were especially needed and recruited by the Ecuadorian government around that time.

• • •

Kane writes that in 1941, there was a war between Ecuador and Peru over the border between the two countries, which is still in dispute. In early 1995, Kane says, there was a battle that lasted more than a week. He notes, "Although no one knows for certain, a strong case has been made that the only thing that stopped the Peruvians from advancing farther was the Huaorani."[77]

...

Why did you want to go?

Because I was patriotic…I wanted to defend my country.

...

Laura Rival mentions that younger generations of Huaorani strongly identify themselves as being Ecuadorian. To them, the outsider, or enemy, is not white people or the Ecuadorian government, but rather, the Peruvians.[78]

In a book published in Ecuador about the Ecuadorian-Peruvian war in 1995, Cecilia Viera Saltos writes:

> "On the southern border, we count on groups of true warriors as capable as they are original. It is these critical moments in which the country lives, where we remember the existence of those men capable of the greatest sacrifice for the defense of Ecuador....Three indigenous shuar [sic] groups, who find themselves in total harmony with the jungle environment with an ancestral bravery, part of a culture

---

[77] Kane, *Savages*, 63.
[78] Rival, *Trekking Through History*, 162.

where courage is a basic element of their lifestyle....These soldiers establish a true communion with the environment, a truly mystical equilibrium, in this world surrounded by spirits of old warriors, of great beasts, or of magic trees."[79]

...

The war taught me to value life more, and to fight for what you want. It made me feel more open-minded.

Fredy says that a lot of the other soldiers were traumatized after the war, after having seen their friends without arms and legs. Everyone, apparently, was sent to a psychiatric clinic for a month after the war to receive treatment.

Had you gone to war before that, in the jungle?

In the jungle, no, I was too young to go.

During the time of the war with Peru, Fredy was still living in Tena. But he felt that he needed to leave, that he needed to go further. He heard that there was a larger world, a city called Quito, the capital of Ecuador, and that there were more cities, too.

"I want to go there," I said. I always wanted to go farther, understand? So I caught a car, and went without any plans. I went like [with] the wind, just carried along.

---

[79] Saltos, *Ecuador en Guerra 1995*.

This was about ten years ago, he says, when he would have been about twenty.

And in Quito, there was more stress. So much that I wanted to return [to Tena].

Where did you stay in Quito?

Oof, one time, I slept in the airport, in the parking lot. Because I didn't know where to go! But I did have money, because I always saved up; I never spent it on alcohol....And later, I went to a small hostel, that was very cheap, about two sucres. I was there, and I felt lonesome...because in a big city, it's very difficult to make friends...And when, one day, I went to the park, Carolina Park, I saw some guys playing ball and asked to join them. Just then, I saw a big plane. "What is that?" I asked them. "A plane," they said. And I asked, "Where do those planes come from?" "Ooh, they come from other countries," they said. "But this one here, is going to Galápagos." "And where is Galápagos?" "It's an island, about six hundred miles from here." "Island?" Because in my dream I saw that I had to go to an island. "And how do I get there from here?" I asked. And they told me, and offered to take me to the airport.

Could you speak Spanish well at that point?

No, not very much. But I was learning fast...the family in Tena spoke Spanish.

Now, Fredy says, for Ecuadorians on the mainland it's very difficult to come to Galápagos, as you can only stay for a limited time and have to state your purpose for going. To limit what has been a rapidly growing population and preserve the famous nature and wildlife on the islands, the government has decided that the only way for Ecuadorians to move to the islands is if they marry someone already living on the Galápagos. Before, when Fredy came, though, you just had to buy your ticket.

When Fredy arrived on the Galápagos, the first thing he did was walk by the waterfront.

I felt like nobody.

Carrying just a small bag of clothing with him, and some money that he'd been saving, he found a cheap hostel. The first job he found was in construction, building houses.

The boss said, "Have you worked in this before?" And I said, "Yes, of course." I always said yes; I never said no.

• • •

According to Robarchek in *Waorani: the Contexts of Violence and War*, there is no simple way to say "I can't" in the Huaorani language. Huaorani can say they refuse to do something, or that they don't want to do something, but not that they are unable to. There is little if any sense of helplessness among members of their tribe.[80]

---

[80] Robarchek, *Waorani*, 119.

Joe Kane has also noted this characteristic. "Because self-sufficiency means so much to the Huaorani," he writes, "the dependency that comes with old age is unacceptable, and the aged often asked to be killed rather than become a burden on their offspring."[81]

• • •

I ask Fredy if there's anything he thinks he doesn't do well and he says no, he can't think of anything. He always likes to tell me what to do—put *ají* on this, no, on the fish, not on the rice, dance like this, this movement....When I point this characteristic out to him, he agrees. "Yes, I'd be a good boss, right?" he says. Playing pool, for instance, it is impressive to watch Fredy's seemingly instinctive, unconscious skill, but sometimes his excessive self-confidence rubs me the wrong way. "Now I kill you," he often says, approaching a shot that he thinks is going to go especially well. Same while playing cards—he always lets you know that he thinks he's the best

Since arriving on the Galápagos, Fredy has worked on fishing boats, in a hotel as a cook, and most recently, on cruise ships as a bartender. He says one of his girlfriends was paying for him to take the necessary courses for him to become a scuba diving instructor, but he never completed them. It wasn't talent that was lacking, he says, but rather motivation. He just wasn't disciplined enough.

---

[81] Kane, *Savages*, 39.

BETWEEN WORLDS

In some ways Fredy's lifestyle on the Galápagos is not very far removed from his jungle past. At first, I thought it must be that Galápagos culture was just so relaxed and that was why Fredy had basically no obligations and could spend most of his time just hanging out and having fun. Talking with some of Fredy's friends, though, I discover that Fredy is uniquely unburdened even for the Galápagos.

Danny Mauricio Becerra Días was one of the first people Fredy met when he arrived on the Galápagos. A slender, medium-tall Latin guy in his late twenties, with an exquisitely carved behind that he says girls from mainland Ecuador have pinched while he was walking in the airport in Quito, Danny is a fisherman, but relatively well-off. He brings over his guitar for me to play for him and Fredy. When I say I need a capo to play one song, Danny offers to hold his finger over the strings on the second fret, and this allows me to play most of the song before he gets too tired—it's great! We end up spending all day in the house, the three of us, playing the guitar, dancing, and playing card games called *mentira* and *burro*. For about forty-five minutes, though, Fredy leaves Danny and me alone so that I can interview him.

Danny says that he met Fredy soon after Fredy arrived on San Cristóbal, because Fredy started playing volleyball with him. The two became friends and started to hang out together because, Danny says,

Fredy "is very chill, and is a good person. A bit *vago*, but a good person."

A little vague? What does that mean?

He's crazy; he never worries...about working, about having material things...that doesn't matter to him.

What about you, are you vague?

No...I work all the time, and I use my money to buy clothes and other things. I have a house, and a yard....I live comfortably, I have a very big house, and a business, too.

Did your parents teach you to live the way you do?

No, I wanted to do things like this....I wouldn't like to live the way Fredy does. I mean, I know he likes how he lives because he lives well; he feels comfortable, and that's fine. But I wouldn't like it. I am always telling Fredy, you have to work, you're already grown up; you are going to have a wife, and children, and you need to have a house, and comforts in your house so that when she goes there, she feels good, you know? It's time; you are getting up there in age and it's time! He says, no, I'm fine like this, that I like living this way, I like to surf, and hang out....

And for you, is that strange? Are there other people like that in San Cristóbal, or is he pretty unique?

Yes, he is pretty unique.

And when Fredy first arrived here, was he the same as he is now, or has he changed?

Yes, he's changed a lot. When he first came here, he was more calm, and a bit humble…he was from the country, so he was more calm. Now, he's a devil.

Fredy lives a life on the Galápagos that is between the savage world and the modern world. While he has a cell phone and wears a Nike hat, Oakley sunglasses, and Columbia and Billabong shirts, the pace of life on the island of San Cristóbal allows him to wake up in the morning worry free, with all day to decide what to do. He can walk on the *muelle*, meet tourists and give surfing lessons, go surfing, drink with friends, or stay inside listening to music or watching television. Later in the evening, there will be Iguana Rock, the bar and disco where Fredy's friends and all of the tourists and volunteers come. A menu of new *gringa* dishes that rotates daily, in the case of the tourists, and weekly or monthly for the volunteers.

While Fredy's life may be even more relaxed than others', the typical Galápagos lifestyle does seem uniquely relaxed compared with the typical lifestyle in the United States or even on mainland Ecuador. As Patricio Hernandez, a young surfer I met at the beach cleanup day, explains, "Look, that is one of the admirable things about the island. Here, there is no need to rob. For what? If you want food, it's easy! You just get a hook, and fish, and you cut it, fry it, and eat it. Or go to *el Alto* [the highlands] and get a banana." Also, he explains, "The person who wants employees, comes and looks for you!" You don't have to go out looking for work.

As various people tell me, there are no storms on the Galápagos, no murder, little theft, and few worries. So different is the Galápagos from more "developed" cultures that presidents and other celebrities who come to visit can walk around without bodyguards. Such illustrious visitors who have walked unrecognized, according to Patricio, include the presidents of Russia and Spain, Marlon Brando, Jennifer Lopez, and Michael Jackson.

One night at Iguana Rock, I had an interesting talk with Danny and Fredy about the cultural differences between the Galápagos and the United States. "In the United States," Danny says, "people are always thinking, how am I going to get to Mars? Whereas here, they are thinking about having children and getting food. They live hour by hour, not always planning for the future." In fact, there's an expression that we use to sum up Galápagos culture, Danny and Fredy tell me: *No se ganan, se gozan*. One doesn't earn, one enjoys. People may be poor on the islands, but Danny thinks people are happier here, with everything *tranquilo*.

A commercial comes on the television in front of the bar, and Fredy and Danny are mesmerized: four marbles suspended from strings, one bounces and another on the opposite side jumps—wow! How do they do that? They ask. Whereas for me and the other foreigners in the bar, the commercial is boring. We have so much stimulation to occupy our minds already. Aren't we in the Galápagos, after all? Fredy and Danny notice my lack of interest, and say, yes, for us, such things are really interesting, because they are new. Television is their method of learning. Here, Danny explains, it's news if an Ecuadorian makes wine, whereas in the United States, heart transplants are commonplace and already no big deal. Yeah, Fredy agrees, here in the Galápagos, we are so fascinated by cell phones, that people who have them get so absorbed looking at them that you can sometimes see them fall into a hole or walk into a lamppost!

Fredy talks about medical treatment as a major difference between the jungle and the modern world. He says that people die young in the jungle because there is no modern medicine. "How could we do a heart transplant in the jungle?" he asks.

And do you think that the methods used now, in modern medicine, are better than plant medicine?

I'm not sure. Now, human life…is more superficial. Like you can walk with a tube in your stomach. They put some tubes here, other tubes there, and bam! Everything changes. You are no longer the original you, but instead a connection of cables and a foot with screws so you can walk. Imagine! Now, life is changing so much that we are going to be robots instead of humans!

We continue our conversation about the differences between Galápagos and European and American lifestyles. In the Galápagos, and on mainland Ecuador, Fredy and Danny note, people have children at fifteen, sixteen, or seventeen, not thirty-two. They want to have more, but a lack of money prevents them. Whereas in Europe, the more money people have, the fewer children they have! Fredy and Danny can't seem to believe this fact. Danny mentions, laughing, that he has heard that

Italy and Switzerland have been trying to get Latin men to come to Europe and make more babies to help with their shortage of children!

On the Galápagos, Danny and Fredy agree, there's an imbalance of men to women of seventy percent to thirty percent. They say it's naturally that way in the *continente*, for instance, in Peru and Colombia. When I press them, they say, no, it's not that more girls die or that they are killed at or before birth, but just, that's the way the percentages come out. Of course, they explain, this causes problems on the island, with women routinely having three or four boyfriends. Foreign girls come to the islands, and it's like a paradise of men for them. In fact, so many *extranjeras* want to stay on the islands that two or three of every group of university students that come do stay. One girl, they recounted, laughing, offered many men $2000 in exchange for marrying her so she could stay here legally. Well, we were suspicious of marrying like that, they said, but she got the ugliest man on San Cristóbal to marry her, and here they are, living here in the town! So many girls from other countries come to San Cristóbal, Danny says, that all the guys have to do is sit and wait. Why travel?

One thing, though, that people are more interested in on the Galápagos, Danny points out, is fashion. They watch and follow the trends closely, just like their favorite soap operas. Whereas for you guys, he says, pointing at me, it doesn't really matter; you're above that. I chew this over for a couple of minutes, and say, yes, maybe it's a circle. Others from super-developed areas of the world and I wanting to return to a more simple lifestyle, while you and others who are used to a more simple lifestyle can't wait to move forward toward a more complex way of living.

Danny explains that life is changing now for Ecuadorians, and even if they wanted to, they could not stop moving forward toward modernity; they need to follow the trend of other countries. *Galápagueños* will not be able to continue having a simple way of life, Danny says. "Why not?" I ask, alarmed.

It is impossible to maintain that simple lifestyle in these times because the other people in the world are prospering and are going up. If we keep staying at the same level, we are going to end up on the floor, and everyone else is going to be on top, with nice houses and lots of money, and we are going to keep on being their slaves, don't you think?

I don't respond.

Sure, because look, if you don't study, and you don't get ahead, you will tend to be a slave...to those who do move upward and have money...That's how I see it.

Still, Danny says, having money is not without its problems. Besides the loss of a simple lifestyle, having a lot of money brings with it theft, and corruption, and pollution, and drugs.... The way it is now on San Cristóbal, there are no murders, no one sells drugs, and "with the little bit that we earn working, we feel happy." If the people on the island had more money, surely there would be more problems, Danny says, because there would be big buildings, and factories, and more cars and big boats, and all of this would ruin the natural life here.

Danny wants to work in conservation, to preserve the natural beauty of the Galápagos. We part ways and Fredy escorts me to my apartment. The next evening, I interview Walter, another person who Fredy says knows him better than others.

Walter Sotomayor has gelled curly hair in a cut that nearly reaches his shoulders. He makes a lot of money, relatively speaking, being a tour guide for large tour groups that come on cruise ships. His English is excellent, but he is not very outgoing and seems more comfortable talking in Spanish so we interview in his native language.

Have you noticed things about Fredy that make him different from other people you know?

Yes, he is a person who lives life as it comes. He lives each day as if it were the last day. He has a very simple lifestyle. He never worries about what is going to happen tomorrow....I think that to some degree, this has a lot to do with where he comes from, with his origins....He doesn't have worries, and I think he is always calm, and relaxed, and content, wouldn't you say? I believe that sometimes one can be very happy with very little. With only the most important things. And the people that have this, the basic necessities, are the happiest people.

Do you think that to some degree, everyone here in Galápagos is like that, free from worries?

No, no, because people here...we are all always creating new needs...like wanting to buy a new television, or a faster car...we create these necessities. If the people were content with what they had, they would be happier.

I ask Walter why it is that Fredy attracts so many *gringas*, but he doesn't offer any guesses. He agrees, however, that the gender imbalance on the island makes it so female volunteers are inundated with interested Latin men. Fredy, not being Latin, is unique among them, even though the *gringas* can't tell his unique jungle heritage straight off. What they do know is that he has a certain charisma, a cuteness, a genuineness, that pulls them to him. Plus, he's a better dancer!

Fredy says his ability to get a lot of girls is part of what makes him a legend here.

How are you able to get with so many girls?

I don't know! Not a lot, a few. They ask me, Billabong, tell me what you have; what do you do to get a girl? I tell them, no, I only speak, I tell them what I am thinking, what I feel, I tell the truth, not lies because lies hurt you….Sometimes I say, listen, I know that I don't know anything. And they say: But, what do you do? You don't have anything! And I reply, that's right, I don't have anything. But I have a heart that is big and strong.

Another time, I ask him again, and he says:

Here, they ask, what do you do to have so many girls? And I say that I am only like the anaconda. I have an instinct, a power, like something magnetic, that just by talking, the girl says, 'wow'. He knows a lot that I want to know. Like you now. You are here, not because I am handsome…You are here with a good purpose that you want to know more about me and I want to know more about you....But, I'm telling you. I have a power, like the anaconda, really. I have a power in my tail, but here no, in my lips...it is a unique attraction that the other guys here don't have. I have my style. I have my gift of being. And that is why I am telling you, te quiero mucho.

Casanova Surfer

Returning to the Galápagos, I was looking forward to experiencing the same passionate, intense dancing with Fredy that I had in 2001. Though we went to Iguana Rock most evenings, however, and there was dancing, only once or twice did I feel the same connection between us on the dance floor. I got frustrated that Fredy did not seem to be communicating in the flow of the movement with me. He seemed distracted, into his own world. Sometimes, he did not even want to dance with me, preferring to play pool and drink beer. Once, we did connect well and we came off the dance floor both dripping with sweat. I could barely walk I was so exhausted, so carried by the spirit of the dance and our connection. But that was the last time I felt that. A few nights later, I complained to Fredy as he walked me back to my room that I wished we had danced more, and he seemed extremely offended. "Am I boring?" he asked me. "Because if I'm boring, then I don't want to be with you anymore."

    The loss of the dance connection between Fredy and me makes me trust him less, and leaves me more nervous about going to the jungle with him. When I tell Fredy that he is making me scared with his comments about feeding me to the anacondas, he grows serious and says that if I don't trust him, he doesn't want to go with me to the jungle. I tell him that I do trust him, because I do want to go to the jungle, but I'm not sure if I really do trust him entirely.

From my interview with Walter Sotomayor:

How does Fredy keep so many girlfriends at the same time?

He must be a very good liar.

Liar. That sounds too strong, perhaps, but Fredy definitely bends the truth on occasion. His mind is not great at keeping details in order, for instance. When we go to purchase airline tickets for our trip to the jungle, later that day Fredy tells one of his friends that we are flying the wrong airline, one of only two that come to the island, and that we are leaving on Friday, when in fact we are leaving on Thursday. Fredy tells the people next door that he will be in the jungle, visiting, for three weeks after I leave for the United States, yet he told me that he's going to Quito after I leave and then coming right back to San Cristóbal. We pass a couple of tourists who are eating outdoors and they call to Fredy, asking him about the waves and when he will be there surfing. Fredy says that he's going at two o'clock, and that he'll see them there. Yet we are at that moment headed in the opposite direction to go snorkeling, so clearly Fredy will not be surfing this afternoon. When I question him, Fredy tells me that he doesn't know who those tourists are and shrugs when I ask him why he told them that.

Fredy's charm makes up for a lot, it seems. The French woman Florence, who was in the apartment next to mine, had commented on how great Fredy and I looked dancing together and asked if she could dance with him next Saturday. Sure, Fredy said, and yet we are not going to be there. It seems like he tells different stories about the same things at different times. For instance, I remember specifically that in 2001, Fredy told me that he had been a guide in the jungle, leading tourists around, yet this year he denied that, saying that perhaps he meant that some Huaorani do that. So when Fredy tells his friends that he is going to feed me to the anacondas and leave me with the piranhas, I laugh but grow nervous, not knowing what to believe.

• • •

Reading Joe Kane's account of his time with Huaorani informant Enqueri, I felt a lot of similarity between his feelings toward Enqueri and mine toward Fredy. Kane noted that Enqueri had very easily wounded pride and did not answer specific questions, such as how long it would take to get somewhere, precisely. Kane writes of Enqueri that one night, "I fell asleep thinking that I liked him very much but that I did not trust him at all."[82]

• • •

I guess it is generally hard for me to trust someone who is a player. Though Fredy's openness about it at least lets me understand his actions better. During several of our interviews, Fredy talks about how he is a girl magnet.

---

[82] Kane, *Savages*, 48.

What can you do if the girls want to be with you?

I can't do anything. Come to the kingdom of Billabong, I say. Come and be part of the flock....

The girls know how I am. I am unique. People realize what I'm like. I'm the same way with everyone. I'm happy, and fun, and I make the girls feel good. I'm always up for anything. Sure! I say. Great, let's go! I am always giving them opportunities to be happy.

You never have to work hard to find girls?

Well, occasionally, for the girls that I really like. But for the rest, it's easy. I just talk, and it's all done.

What, follow me to my bed?

Follow me to my bed, there it is. Not to my bed first, to my room, first, my living room. Wine first, and then whisky....

With all of his experience with foreign tourists, Fredy has drawn some conclusions about the world's females:

The most liberal girls are from Europe. The easiest girls are from Switzerland. The most difficult, are from Israel and Denmark...I've actually never had a girl from those countries...And from what I've seen, the craziest girls are from Holland. And the coldest girls are from Germany. They are cold in all aspects. And the girls that are most focused, he said, with a pointed glance at me, *are those from Harvard.*

Fredy recounts the first things he learned to say in English. Of course, they were very useful to his island lifestyle:

Very good. What's your name? Do you have a boyfriend? You like Galápagos? How old are you? Where are you from? Can I go out with you? We come to walk on the beach....Can I kiss you?

Fredy says to me, "*Te quiero mucho,*" which I take to mean that he cares about me and likes me a lot. And yet I never feel that I can take him completely seriously because of my knowledge, from friends of his and from his own stories, of his romantic involvement with so many other girls, *gringas,* and many at the same time. Fredy tells me about a couple of times when he composed a lovey-dovey email to one foreign girlfriend, and accidentally sent it to a different one. "She was so mad!" he says, laughing.

Once, Fredy says, he sent an email meant for me to another girl named Madeline, and she said she would forgive him that one time. But in the past, he has done that to Celine, Anne, and others,[83] and they have broken up with him. Fredy seems to think that if the girls really love him, they will forgive him, that everyone makes mistakes. I feel really uncomfortable hearing this, as in my mind having ten *novias* at the same time is a lot worse than a simple mistake of misdirecting an email.

---

[83] Names have been changed to protect privacy.

I don't understand why you want so many girls...

It's that [in the jungle], you have to do this so that you don't lose your last name. You have to have a lot of children so that your last name will last for many generations. That is why you have lots of wives, to have plenty of children. So [the man's] last name doesn't get lost.

Because the man is more important than the woman?

Yes, in the jungle, yes....Here, I'll settle for two wives.

Is there a philosophy in the jungle that if you work hard, you will earn a reward, or something like that? Do people value work in itself?

Yes, there you get an Oscar. [He laughs.] No, there, when you are a very hard worker, or a good fisherman, the girls want you. If you are capable, the girls desire you. Guys who know a lot, and who know how to do everything, are desired. That's why all the girls like me.

Fredy often goes back to the fact that he was going to be able to have multiple wives as *cacique* in the jungle, and I ask him how he feels about just having one wife here in the Galápagos, as is the custom in most other places in the world. "It's okay," he says, "but I feel capable of having at least two here." "Capable? Capable in what sense?" I ask him.

I feel capable of being with two wives. Like in Arab countries, they have four or five wives.

What do you mean by "capable"? Capable of providing food for them, or of being with them physically?

Yes, physically, in terms of love, I feel capable. Because, I don't know, I feel that I can make both of them happy. That's the feeling I have. And I've done it, too....

Fredy tells me of a time when he was physically romantic with three girlfriends at the same time.

Were you in love with all of them?

Yes. I don't know, I have a big heart for loving. I felt good with them...I am always the same person...always very open. I would talk to each of them like they were the only one.

Fredy says once he was in bed with two of these girlfriends, Madeline and Janet, at same time. A new experience for them and for him as well.

The three of us were like a single body. And I was the sole king....But now, no, times have changed. I have realized that here, in this society, I can't have three or four women—big problems.

Fredy explains that in the jungle, the wives live together.

One cooks, another watches the children, another goes to work on the chacras,[84] and the other might be pregnant....

---

[84] small plots of cultivated land

And the wives don't fight?

No. They are not jealous in the jungle. Because of this, I think that here they will not be jealous, when in fact they are. I have realized that here, women are jealous, and that I can't have a lot at the same time any more.

If I have a lot of women, I feel like, wow, the king.

How did it work in the jungle—the husband was with a different wife each night?

Something like that. There it's not like all of the wives want to have sex every night, no. It always changes. Now it's your turn, now it's yours...and there was never a preference for one in particular.

There's never a preference?

No, in love everyone is equal.

How is it possible not to have a preference?

....It's like here, for me: if all of the girls are nice, who am I going to give preference to? I can't.

Fredy says that love does exist in the jungle, but that it forms over time, after a married couple has been together for a while. In the Galápagos, Fredy had to learn a totally different concept of love. Here, he meets couples that have been together for four or five years, and still aren't married. "How is that possible?" he asks me. "How can they be together for that long and still not have children?"

In the words of Mimanca, one of Lino Tagliani's Huaorani informants:

> A man and a woman without children are like two dry branches: When a dry branch falls from a tree, we pick it up and burn it. Life without children is like being dead. How can one live without communicating life?[85]

...

In the jungle, making love means you are going to get married. As a result, Fredy says, he never had sex in the jungle. According to him, he had sex for the first time six years ago, at age twenty-four, with a girl from Switzerland who *"le hizo el amor"*—made love to him. When the *suisa* made love to him, a light turned on in his head—ah! Women. He was very shy, and didn't know what to do. He'd never kissed anyone before! He fell in love with the girl, completely, and was devastated when she left, because for him, making love with someone meant that she was going to be your wife. Fredy says that the Swiss girl wasn't in love with him, though. When I ask him why the girl wanted to be with him, Fredy says, because I was different from the other *chicos*, not out to grab the girls and have sex; he was somewhat apart from that. He says he danced a little at that point, but not super well.

According to Fredy, there is a *casa de citas* here on the island—a whore house, and that after arriving

---

[85] Tagliani, *También el Sol Muere*, 152.

on the Galápagos and partying with people, guys tried to convince him to go, asking him if he'd ever had sex, and Fredy pretended like yes, sure, he had had a lot of sexual experiences, but that he didn't want to go. He hadn't! The real reason he didn't want to go, he says, is that he felt timid about it.

Here in the Galápagos, Fredy says, people have sex as young as twelve or thirteen. In addition, it's very common here that very young people go to prostitutes or are prostitutes themselves. In the jungle, though, he says it's more like eighteen or twenty, whenever you first get married. (This seems too old to me for a savage tribe, but maybe that's just prejudice talking.)

In the jungle, you don't kiss. You see monkeys kissing a little, "mua mua," on the eyes, but kissing is something I learned about here.

How many novias *have you had?*

Ten.

(I don't trust that, of course.)

The longest time I've had a girlfriend was two or three months, no more. And the shortest was one night.

With all these girls, are you always looking for love, or just fun?

I don't know, I've never talked with a girlfriend about the future, about getting married, but...I am open to everything. If it's just for fun, it's just fun. If it's something real, it's something real. If it's something more serious, it's more serious. I always have the doors open, an open mind.

All this talk about sex has gotten me feeling really annoyed—Fredy telling me how he's had sex with one *chica* and another *chico*, then with another couple...."*Estoy abierto a todo*," he says; I'm open to everything. Yet, when I asked Fredy if there's something he would never do, he said, have sex with a gay man. Fredy says he has met female tourists who say they are lesbians, and he doesn't approve of that. I ask why he has such strong feelings about this, if he's already had sex with a man with another woman, but he doesn't answer. He also says he doesn't think he wants to have sex with a black girl.

• • •

In contrast to Fredy's strong views, Robarchek thinks that homosexual sex is acceptable and common among the Huaorani. "Among men," he writes, "…it seems that, when it comes to sex, the gender of the partner is largely irrelevant."[86]

• • •

Do you think you are ready to get married?

I'm not sure, but I want to see what it's like.

You want to try it out?

---

[86] Robarchek, *Waorani*, 106.

If I get married, I could always get divorced later.

Do you prefer the custom in the jungle of having a lot of wives, or the system here?

It's a bit difficult here, because here, you can only have one wife, right?

Mmmhmm.

But I can't have just one wife.

Why not?

Because I come from an ascendancy of having four or five wives.

...

Another time, when I ask Fredy which system of love and marriage he prefers, he says that he prefers the one now, that of trying to find the ideal woman for him, rather than marrying someone he barely knows and hoping that love will form.

"But," he says, "it is difficult finding the right person."

Do you think you are going to find the person?

Yes, actually I've already found her, but she's leaving at the end of the month.

Fredy and the author in Fredy's room, 2005

ISLAND LIFE

I want to hear more about Fredy from others. How does he fit in on the Galápagos? Is he more like a local, or a foreigner? From the time I've spent with him on San Cristóbal, I see that Fredy is not afraid to share his jungle heritage with others. He has certain phrases, for instance, that he likes to toss out, such as "I eat everything that moves—so don't move!" or, "Jungle surfing!" Funny the first few times, but since I hear Fredy tell them over and over again, they become kind of tiresome.

I have told some friends about my life. They say that I am the legend of Galápagos…..Because I am from over there, I have come to be a legend here. Because…I have a gift of being very friendly. I can be with the most vicious person, but with him, I am good.

Do you tell everyone you meet that you're from the jungle?

Yes, everyone. "Jungle surfing."

So everyone here on San Cristóbal knows a bit about your story, then?

Yes, I've told them, but they're not that interested.

When I ask him if there are any other people from tribes here on San Cristóbal, Fredy says no, here the people are from the coast, and from Quito. I ask again if there are other indigenous people here, and he says he's not sure, maybe on Santa Cruz Island. Here, that he knows of, no.

When the local people look at you, do they know that you are different from them, or not?

They only know that I am a person with a good heart. That I don't go doing bad things, like stealing, fighting in the street, or like with girls....With girls, they know that, yes, I know a lot of people....(glances sheepishly at me)...Well, not that many.

But, do you, physically, look different from them, do you think?

I have my own style.

    Besides his surfing buddies and a couple of other friends, Fredy seems to be always hanging out with foreigners. Perhaps because he himself is like a foreigner? Once, I wanted to dance and he took me to Neptuno, a *discoteca* that attracts more locals than foreigners, and Fredy seemed a bit uncomfortable. When I ask him why he prefers Iguana Rock to Neptuno, he replies:

It's that all of my people are there. All of my friends...What are you going to do in Neptuno? Dance, and dance, and dance? I prefer to talk a little, play pool, watch television, see new people, meet new people, and teach salsa.

Fredy and friends at Iguana Rock

In 2001, Scuba Bar on the main front road by the piers was the happening place for tourists, locals, and volunteers, but that, along with the two *discotecas* next to it, are now closed, made into a tourist shop and ice cream store. The new popular hangout is a bar called Iguana Rock, which has an intimate, living room party feel, with a television, couches, a bar, a pool table, and a small dance floor with basic flashing lights and a fog machine. The place is not focused so much on dancing, but has more of a bar-type setup that makes me feel more awkward. It has only a small dance floor that is positioned in a prominent position so that if you go up there, everyone's eyes are on you.

On my first visit to Iguana Rock, a white guy with a slight paunch and curly brown hair comes in with two German volunteers. He starts to play pool with Fredy, and wow is he good. He comes over to me and asks, in English, "Do you remember me?" "No," I tell him. "I remember you," he says, and proceeds to tell the two girls he is with how I was here a few years ago and came back from Española Island completely green and unable to walk, and how he was on the dock when I arrived. "It was as though you were drunk!" he says. I laugh, flattered that he would remember me and have such a good memory. Victor, his name is—I do remember the name, and notice that he fills out the front of his jeans very nicely and is confident without sounding cocky. Victor runs a scuba diving school in town and is very adept seeming, a good dancer, too. My interview with him is the only one from this project conducted in English, and he has plenty of insights to offer.

Do you think Fredy fits in well with the people here?

Yeah, he's the famous Billabong here; he's a celebrity here!

Why's he a celebrity?

He's the Billabong, you know, the surfer, the gringa hunter, *the cool guy...everyone likes Billabong. Nobody hates Billabong. I don't see anyone hating Billabong....*

In addition to a wall of his room decorated with postcards from friends around the world, Fredy shows me a journal where he collects messages from people who have passed through San Cristóbal and spent time with him. Everyone thanks him for being so generous and for showing them a wonderful time. They write that he has a big heart, that he's a great dancer, that they'll never forget him. That he's taught them a lot about life.

When I was talking with Andres Moriano...we were saying one day, we must do a book about Billabong. I mean this is a celebrity, we need to do something like that..."Billabong, the Galápagos Surfer"...something like that.

• • •

Fredy is extremely generous, and people can tell he has a good heart just by looking at him. As a result, people give him all sorts of things, and he also freely shares and gives his own things out to others. Fredy tells me about a time that he was in Quito and Guayaquil with one of his girlfriends, and he was giving food to children on the street. He said he argued with his girlfriend about that, how he was spending his money on giving rather than on securing needs for himself.

• • •

I want to tell you something about my friend. He's a good guy. Very much a good guy. And, sometimes he's naïve, about many things, but I never saw him do something evil. Never....People here can be evil, talking bad about people on purpose, but I never saw him do something evil to somebody. He has a good heart.

What sorts of things is he naïve about?

Yeah...sometimes he trusts too much in the people, and people do bad things to him. Rob stuff from him. Sometimes the local guys are not very nice. That's why, I have not many friends, but the friends I have are good friends, like

Billabong, for example. He's open; he's like a good momma. It's like, if somebody needs help...he never says no to his friends, never. That's why sometimes the people abuse him and rob stuff and stuff like that.

Do you think he's better off here?

If he goes to the mainland, he will be destroyed there. The people in the mainland are really evil. And he's too naïve to live in Guayaquil or Quito. They're gonna kill him. I mean, he's gonna have a bad time over there. Billabong, no, he belongs here. He belongs to San Cristóbal. Maybe another place, like this, but not a big city. They're gonna kill him; they gonna eat him alive....He needs to have this evilness, to see, when it's bad...recognize if something happens....He don't have that. He's too naïve in that way.

Well, he knows how to adapt pretty well, right?

I mean, he can adapt to some things, but he's never gonna adapt to the evilness of the people. I don't see him...do something like that. I don't believe he can manage that situation.

• • •

In 1994, the Texas-based oil company Maxus issued a manual to its employees working in Ecuador, instructing them as to how to deal with a Huaorani encounter:

> "All contacts with the Waorani should be avoided. However, if you have an unforeseen encounter with a Wao, keep

calm....Do not show fear or make any gesture that might seem aggressive. Tell the Wao that you are his friend and, looking at his face, repeat these words: 'Waponi, amigo Waorani, boto Maxus.' (Greetings, Waorani friend, I am Maxus.")"[87]

...

On the third or fourth day of my visit, Fredy realized that an acquaintance he'd invited over to his apartment after the *discoteca* the previous night left with his $150 Oakley sunglasses. He got very upset and looked like he might cry, saying that this always happens to him—he always opens his house to people and they take things from him.

A week later, Fredy came to my place for dinner, looking relieved and jittery. He told me how he had seen the guy who had taken his sunglasses, and that he was wearing the sunglasses on his head. Luckily, Fredy said, he saw the guy before the guy saw him, so he was able to snatch the glasses back rather than having to confront him verbally first. "I was so nervous to take back the glasses!" he said. "But then I told the guy that they were mine and he said okay. I was so relieved!" With such a response, it seems ironic that Fredy is part of the feared Huaorani tribe.

Do you think some people are jealous of Fredy?

---

[87] Maxus Ecuador, Inc., "Bleeding Heart of Darkness," 20–21.

Yeah, many people are jealous, but not like in the bad way...Because many young guys like to be with many girls, like him. And definitely, if he wants, he get the girl....He have this charm, you know...so, that's good for him. I'm happy for him....He's naughty with the girls, like, you know, very naughty, but as a friend, he's a good friend. He don't hesitate; he don't doubt it. If he needs to protect me, he's going to do it.

Why do you think Fredy attracts so many gringas?

Because he's cute....He's not the most handsome guy in the world, but his personality is cute, and that's why he attract gringas. *His dance....and playing pool, and laughing all the time—he's never pissed off. I never saw him pissed off, never, ever in my life. He's always smiling...sometimes he's worried, but never pissed off. That attracts the girls very much, I think.*

*Billabong have like four chances to leave—girls from Switzerland, go to embassy, pay ticket...and he don't go. He still here. And one of these girls, she was a dream. She was so cute. She was one of my diving students. She looks like a model....I was like, Billa**bong**!*

He's a Switzerland girl specialist. But he still here; he don't go.

Do you think he's afraid of settling down?

Probably. I think he's afraid to move away from here. I think he feels that this is his house. His home, with his friends. Because we take care of us....We have a small group of friends...we hang out in different places, but if something happens, we…take care of each other…Andrés, Victor, Billabong, Martín, Juan Carlos…we take care of ourselves.

For instance, Victor says, they wouldn't let one another sleep in the street.

Do you think he's changed in the time you've known him?

Yeah, of course; he's getting mature. He's getting old, like me. We've known each other for six years, and I've seen him different from now. Now…at that time, he was like [a] wild guy, looking for girls all the time, for fun, for parties, for drinking…he doesn't drink that much now. He's drinking a lot less, and he's more concerned about working. So I think it's much better.

As we continue to talk, the tourists from the day's snorkeling expedition are coming back to the diving house to change out of their rented wetsuits. Victor is distracted, then continues:

He need to learn a lot of things. He come from this society in the jungle, you know; he's…real indigenous, from the jungle, and come to the Galápagos for surfing?! It's a big change for him.

•••

When I first came to the Galápagos in 2001, Fredy was living in a hotel right near my house called the San Cristóbal, and I remember that he told me he was able to have the room in exchange for helping out the owner. I now find out that the owner actually left

Fredy in charge of the hotel while he was away, so apparently the place, under Fredy's touch, acquired quite a reputation as a party and marijuana spot. Victor mentions that four years ago, in the days of the hotel, he and Fredy and their friends were drunk every day.

Yeah, what was that like, [in the hotel]?

That was cool, because in that time, there was not that much work here...airplanes didn't come here too often...so basically, we don't have a job, because we have the shop, but nobody comes, so we are like out of money, so the thing we do with Andrés, is...remember, Billabong had a small green canoe, in the back of the hotel, so every day, we go to the canoe, and go fishing. We buy the hooks and the nylon, and go fishing. We get four, five fish, and we go and have a barbecue....Billabong find...green bananas to make patacones, *rice, and something to drink, and we eat every day like that, because we don't have money....We living in his hotel...that was so crazy.*

It seems like while I was away at Harvard, Fredy was sharing his past lifestyle with friends, showing *Galapagueños* how to live Amazon style!

WITHOUT NEED

Fredy has always been very generous toward me, bringing me flowers, cleaning up when I made dinner, and one morning, preparing for me an elaborate plate of sliced fruit in concentric circles, topped with a pink rose-like flower. He tells me how one time, for a girlfriend who was coming to visit him, he covered his entire room, bed, floor, bench, and shelves, with rose petals. "I killed her," he says, smiling at the memory.

A week into my stay, around lunchtime, I say to Fredy, "Let's go eat; I'm hungry." But looking up at me, he tells me that he can't. He's run out of money. I can't believe this since he has seemed to be very generous in spending money in the last week. He bought me a necklace for my arrival, and he was spending money on gum and renting movies while I was with him.

Why did you spend money on *chicle* and movies, I ask, if you were going to run out? He doesn't quite answer, but basically, Fredy likes to take one moment at a time—he still thinks a bit like in the jungle, eat what and when you can. Fredy is politely reluctant, but I get him to accept my offer to treat him to lunch. He is supposed to get money from some woman at the hotel who comes back on Saturday, but we'll see if that actually happens. I can't imagine living like that, not knowing where your next meal is coming from!

A couple of days later, Fredy admits that he waits until he has no more money to find a job, works for a while, and then does not work until he needs to. I ask him, what would he do if he needed to have an operation? Die? And he says, yes, I suppose I would die. To tell you the truth, I never thought about that.

...

Kane observes that when the Huaorani have food, they eat everything in sight. At one point during his trip, Kane asked his Huao companion Quemperi, "Shouldn't we save some for later?" and Quemperi responded, "Later? What is 'later'?"[88] Kane notes that the Huaorani do not think of hunting until they are starving. "...long-term planning is not what the Huaorani do well, or, for that matter, at all."[89] He describes, too, that whenever a Huao would receive any money, from being a boatman for tours, working for an oil company, or selling a blowgun or a spear, he would invite other Huaorani to come with him to a restaurant in Coca and spend everything buying fried chicken and sodas for them. Kane explains, however: "This was not profligacy: The Huaorani ideal is to be independent and self-reliant, and every effort is made to give the appearance, at least, of being so clearly in tune with the abundance of the forest that one is without fear of need."[90] The generosity of giving away food shows that this person is in this ideal state of being without need.

---

[88] Kane, *Savages*, 37.
[89] Kane, *Savages*, 54.
[90] Kane, *Savages*, 19.

Perhaps Huaorani generosity is similar to the kind of generosity displayed in *potlatches*, elaborate feasts traditionally held by the Kwakiutl and other Northwest Coast Native American tribes, at which people would give away huge quantities of food and valuable gifts in order to establish their social rank. The more they were able to give away, the more powerful it showed them to be.

...

Back in the Galápagos, however, this money thing has me feeling uncomfortable—a few days was one thing, but a week and a half, plus the trip to the *selva*...I really don't understand how Fredy can function like this—he missed getting his money from his boss when she was here Saturday, and is going to try to catch her in Quito, on our way to the jungle, but he doesn't sound at all sure that he'll be able to find her.

Meanwhile, Fredy asks me to lend him a dollar so he can take a taxi to his surf spot, and then after dinner says he is going to buy a *tabaco*. I stop. How, I say, do you have money for cigarettes if you don't have any for food? He says he has *diez centavos*, and I say, with that you can buy an egg, some bread, or a banana. He laughs, as though what I am saying is strange or funny.

At Iguana Rock, later, I buy a beer and a water for us, but Fredy mooches beer and cigarettes from his friends the whole evening (perhaps not as much as normal, but oof!). Times like these really make me wonder how I was drawn to Fredy in the first place.

TIGERS AND ANACONDAS

Fredy tells me that in the jungle there is a large female fish called *bujeo*, and that when you take out its fat and make this into a cream with medicinal plants, it has the power to make another person fall madly in love with you. But only temporarily. The fish creates a big illusion that lasts for one week. You may not even know the person, but suddenly you're crying because you want to marry him. But afterwards, if the person does not give you the cream again, you hate the person you just swooned over, and don't want to see even their photo. Some people use this fish formula to marry others. Fredy says that when he returned to the jungle, he looked for this cream, but wasn't able to find any. "Have you ever used this fish?" I ask. "Yes, on you the first time that I met you."

...

About a year after I met him, Fredy tells me, he returned to the jungle to visit his family and to search for the special *bujeo* cream that induces others to fall in love with you. He visited his family for about two weeks, and he has pictures of himself with his brother and with his brother's anaconda around his neck. I have a hard time believing that he returned, and that the anaconda around his neck in the photo was actually his pet back when he was a child. When I ask Fredy whether his parents were happy to see him, his face grows sad and it seems like he might cry. "It was a little strange," he says. "Were they angry with you for leaving the jungle?" I ask. And his silence indicates to me that something to that effect is true.

When he's thinking about his parents is not the only time I see Fredy sad. Sometimes when I arrive at his apartment in the morning he is lying on his bed, listening to a slow, plaintive ballad. He tells me that he has been crying. When I ask him why, he says that he has everything, and yet he has nothing. He feels lonesome. The foreign friends and girlfriends that he meets always leave, he says, like I will, too. People coming and going, passing through, as if Fredy's world is a theme park, not a home.

Seeing Fredy sad, I start to feel sad, and guilty, too, for I know that I am yet another transient visitor to Fredy's theme park. While I truly value my relationship and interactions with Fredy, it is also true that I have other motives for so actively trying to understand his life. For instance, I know that I am interested in going back to the jungle with him for the purposes of my documentary project. As the trip approaches, Fredy seems to enjoy telling me about all the dangers in the jungle and teasing me about how I am going to get eaten.

Anacondas are in the swamps, with a head the size of a basketball. They can eat a human as if it were a pill.

I ask if the anacondas have done this with anyone from his tribe, and he says that yes, some people have disappeared and it is assumed that they were eaten by anacondas.

It's especially dangerous when you are fishing in a river with a stick, because there the anaconda can hypnotize you. They have a power, like a magnet, that attracts you. It's like a magnet in their tails; you are just there fishing with a hook made of fish or animal bone, and when the anaconda is there, he goes around in circles, and the movement of his body makes the water rise, like the sea. But you don't notice because you're busy fishing more fish, and then the anaconda comes up to you and grabs you around the ankle with his tail. His tail is like a hook, very hard so that you can't escape, and drags you into the river.

If the anaconda sees you first, Fredy explains, you are easy prey. But if you see the anaconda first, you can escape, because you know that he wants to eat you. Anacondas are dangerous not only in the rivers, Fredy says, but also when you are walking through the jungle, because they are inside of brushwood and leaves, and at midday, they enter into a deep sleep, so deep that you can touch them and they won't stir. This lasts for one hour, until one in the afternoon. But after their nap, if they see you first, it's bad news.

The anaconda looks at you and casts a spell so that you walk and end up going in circles…the anaconda hypnotizes you so that you can't find your way, and then you get really tired, and you sit down, and go to sleep. And then the anaconda comes, wraps its body around yours, and drags you to the water, where it's easier for them to eat you. They are from the water.

Why don't the anacondas just eat you immediately, when they first see you?

Because they know that you will leave...they know that you will think of the danger. They have their method of hunting, and they can even imitate animals, birds, and other things. They can make the sounds of birds and animals, making the animals think that they are one of their young and come close. They make different sounds depending on how hungry they are. If they want to eat dessert, a bird sound. If they want to eat lunch, maybe a deer. And if they want something even more tasty, a human cry.

The anaconda Fredy had as a pet as a child didn't eat him because it was a land anaconda, he explains, which only eats small birds. The water anacondas eat anything they encounter, and come out on land only for two reasons: to sunbathe, or because they are hungry.

If the anacondas eat you, after three or four days, they throw up, because they don't eat meat, only blood. They take you into their stomachs, suck out all of your blood, and they get rid of you. When you see the body on the shore, you see the whole body but covered with a white foam, and punctured with small holes all over.

Fredy emphasizes that the anaconda has magical powers that no other animal has.

If you kill an anaconda, you have to take the head with you, because otherwise the body of the anaconda will rejoin.

Once, he says, his family cut up an anaconda in pieces and buried the head a little ways away. When they returned, they found the whole body of the anaconda back together, all clean, and just above where the head was buried, as though the body had been looking for its head.

...

Maybe Fredy was so skilled at making a good time of foraging for food and relaxing in the days of the hotel because he had so much experience doing both in the jungle. With just a week left before we are to head off there ourselves, I ask Fredy more about what life was like in the Amazon.

How did you measure time there?

There we are guided only by the sun. And when the sun is not out, at five a.m., we listen for birds that sing. At midday, a different bird sings. And in the afternoon, a different bird sings. There are different bird whistles for five a.m., lunch and dinner.

What is conversation like in the jungle? Is there conversation?

Yes, but it's about fishing, hunting, how to fish, how you can hunt an animal, things like that.

It was a big deal for Fredy to see the sea when he came to the Galápagos. Looking out at the water, he thought it must be like a big river. For his family in the jungle, after all, there was no notion of an outside world. The jungle was everything.

We thought that it was only us.

Did you have any conception of the world, with the sun?

I'm not sure. There, people live just to live. Not to be famous or important, to have luxuries or big things, understand? There, it was just fishing, hunting, and children.

As Adrian Warren writes, "The Waorani idea of the world is very simple: a flat disc of forest with mountains (the Andes) on one side. Down the centre flows a river, the water of which is recirculated round the edge of the disc to flow through once more."[91]

Was there a belief in other worlds, like in the sky?

Only in the moon, the full moon. And also, sometimes when there were solar eclipses, we thought that the sun god was angry.

Were there other gods?

Really just those two, the sun and moon.

Fredy explains that they used whistles and bird sounds to call to one another to confirm that your friend was nearby and not an enemy or a tiger. You can't shout in the jungle, Fredy says, because that would scare the animals and the people you want to attack, so instead you use the sounds of the jungle. Fredy also says that he had to run a lot in the jungle,

---
[91] Warren, "Waorani."

away from tigers.⁹² That's why, he explains, he had more muscle in his legs in the jungle, whereas now he has more in his back and arms from surfing. In the jungle, a tiger would approach your footprints, put its paw in, and if the print was warm, the tiger would leave you alone, because it meant that you were healthy. If your print did not have warmth, though, it meant you were sick or weak and then the tiger, knowing you were easy prey, would follow you. To protect children against tigers, Fredy tells me that Huaorani adults would put a hot pepper called *ají* in their childrens' eyes. The heat from the *ají* would spread to all parts of their body, so their prints would be warm for the tiger's inspection.

The ají was very strong, and gave you warmth, so that when the tiger placed his paw in your footprint, he would feel your energy and not think that you were easy prey.

The Huaorani would also examine tracks closely to gather information. Fredy says that like the tigers, he and his tribe knew how to smell or feel animal and human tracks, to tell how long ago a creature was there.

We're always looking all around us, and always with our ears wide open.

I ask Fredy if they had knives in the jungle, and he says no, that they used special flat stones.

---

⁹² Fredy uses the word *tigre* but perhaps he means jaguar, like I found references to in research.

Isn't it hard on the feet to walk in the jungle without shoes?

No. But sometimes, if you step on a snake that bites, you have to tie your leg and suck out the poison, because if you don't, you die.

While we are walking on the rocky path to his surfing spot one day, Fredy gets a splinter in his foot. Without a second's hesitation, he grabs a thin branch of a tree and breaks it so that it makes a perfect point, roots around in his foot and out pops the splinter.

And you know how to avoid all of these dangers?

Of course.

How did you learn?

When I was fourteen or fifteen, I went with my parents to hunt...I learned to observe animal tracks and read from them how long ago they were there, where they could be now...also to tell what plants and fruits were poisonous and which weren't.

Despite these abilities that he describes, Fredy says that in comparison with the Galápagos, in the jungle, "you don't use your head so much"

There, you use strength...to run, to hunt, to be very agile. But here, no. Here it is a different type of strength. Here, the strength [needed for surfing] is desire, style, and dedication. But not in the jungle.

Jungle Surfing

Surfing, Fredy has told me, is a high-risk game, because with one false move you can easily slice yourself up on the rocks. "It was like a drug, a high, that I am still addicted to," he says.

But, there are a lot of dangers in the jungle, more than in surfing, right? What about the anacondas?

As Patzelt writes, "I have never encountered an elderly Huao; there is a very high percentage of people who die in wars, in accidents, or because of parasites, malnutrition, snake bites, etc."[93]

I think that there is more danger surfing than in the jungle.

When I ask Fredy whether his childhood in the jungle helps him in surfing at all, he replies that yes, because he learned how to swim in the rivers there. In the jungle, though, he explains, you don't really know how to swim, you just do the doggy paddle. Whereas in the Galápagos, he learned how to "really" swim, with the strokes athletes use.

In 2001, Fredy told me something about surfers that really impressed me. "To be a surfer," he said, "you need to be agile of both mind and body." Now, Fredy admits that some of his agility as a surfer does come from the jungle, where he had to be nimble and

---

[93] Patzelt, *Los Huaorani*, 96.

alert to walk, swing on vines, and climb trees. To jump from one place to another, like to escape quicksand. He explains that surfing uses a lot of instinct, but that, *"Las olas te dan para que seas agil:"* the waves give you what you need to be agile.

If you don't jump, you can fall and die. So, you either jump, or you stay. It's like they say in surfing, "Go big or go home." So, what do I do? I go big.

Surfing is not all related to the jungle, though—it's also connected to the Internet. Fredy says that he and the other surfers are always checking the Internet to see when the big waves are going to arrive. Apparently, they arrive first in Hawaii, and then in the Galápagos. He says he doesn't really like checking the waves on the Internet, but that is the way to catch the best ones.

Fredy returning from an afternoon surfing

...

Humberto Hernandez knows Fredy from surfing and was one of the first people to surf in the Galápagos. The surfing in the Galápagos is great, he says, because here you can surf with animals, like sea lions, turtles, and sharks, and it's not crowded like Peru or California. Humberto considers Fredy a good friend and a good surfer, who, if he dedicated himself, could become a champion. "How does Fredy survive without working very much?" I ask him. "I think that his girlfriends take care of him. He works once in a while, for two or three months, and then relaxes for seven months."

...

Perhaps in part because Fredy easily befriends people and is well cared for, many of his comments suggest that he thinks that his past life in the jungle was inferior to the life he leads here. Whereas my outsider assumption, back in 2001, for instance, was that Fredy was a sensual dancer because his jungle past put him closer in touch with the rhythms of nature, Fredy seems to think that everything he knows about music and dance he learned in the Galápagos. Didn't they have any instruments or dancing in the jungle, I ask him?

Only the drum, a type of flute, and other instruments made from gourds, called pepas de monte, *that hang on a cord. They only used these things at ceremonies, he says, not in daily life.*

Did people in your tribe sing or whistle?

Well, more like shouts, like "eheyeheyeheheheh," during ceremonies, with the dance around the fire. Not at other times.

...

Elisabeth Elliot, wife of speared SIL missionary Jim Elliot, who continued working in the Huaorani territory after her husband's death, also observed a lack of music among the Huaorani. She noticed at one point that the dancing and drum beating of the Quechua women "baffled the Auca women, who knew no musical instruments."[94] Kane begs to differ, however, mentioning that the Huaorani sing knowledge of their territory and where to find things like medicine down through generations.[95]

...

You're saying you didn't know about rhythm, for moving your body, before coming to the Galápagos? I ask Fredy skeptically. No, he says. The only kind of dance we did in the jungle was more like jumping than dancing. Here, the dancing is so much better, he says, because it lets him differentiate himself as a Latin man. Fredy says that because he is now part of the culture on the Galápagos, he likes what the people here like. He has changed his likes to correspond with his environment. Yet, Fredy admits

---

[94] Elliot, *The Savage, My Kinsman*, 33.
[95] Kane, *Savages*, 234.

that his lifestyle on San Cristóbal is different from that of other people on the island, because, in his words, whereas they live, with a house, and a car, he only survives. He only has the necessities. "I have to do everything myself; no one helps me," he says. And I don't really understand his meaning.

But, you have fewer obligations and things than the majority of the people here, no?

Yes.

And why might that be? Because you are from the jungle?

That could be. Because look, I sometimes use the same instinct from the jungle. In the jungle, I didn't do anything. Here, I work for two or three months, and then I stop for five months. I want...to feel more free....I want to feel like I'm in the jungle. It's like, with you. I don't have to do anything. Sometimes, surf, or go to the beach, play volleyball, go drinking if I want to, like that.

So, your past in the jungle has made you different from other people, then?

Yes, different. Because here, the people think in a different manner, because they're from the island....I have learned from them, to be more open, be more, like, what's up, how's it going, what are you up for, ok, let's go—like that. And now I know how to be that way. That couldn't happen in the jungle....What could it be? Let's go to the beach, let's pick up some girls...how could that be? **There, there is nothing.** *What are you going to say? Let's go to the river, or to the vines? Nothing else. We can't say, let's go to the* *dance club, to the bar, cool, let's go, we're going to see this, we're going to speak English....*

Do you think people are happier in the jungle or outside the jungle?

Me, now, outside the jungle.

But...

But before, everything was tranquil; you just lived your life, and there you can have like two wives, two or three.

And your father had several?

Yes...There you have three, except the cacique, *who is like a king, he can have five wives.*

Your father was the cacique?

Of course. And me too, I almost had five wives.

LOBERÍA LEGEND

My final interview on San Cristóbal Island is with Giovanny Sarigu, one of Fredy's closest friends, and the only one besides Victor whom I remember from my time on the island four years before. I recall that Giovanny was good looking, a bit younger than Fredy, and that he was impressed back then when he saw me dance. I am especially excited to interview him because he has mentioned to me that he considers Fredy to be his idol.

You mentioned last night that he is your idol, or something like that.

Yes, yes.

Why is he your idol?

Because he is surprising. Look, every day I worry about working, and if I don't work, I can't live. Because I have a lot of things to pay for....But he is surprising....He leads such a simple life...like a bird, never worrying about what he is going to eat tomorrow....He survives. He is relaxed, he enjoys life, and he has very good friends. He has good girls too; he is never alone, so that's great, right?

Could you have a life like that?

No, I couldn't.

Why not?

Giovanny with Fredy at Punta Carola

Because I know other things that are different. Ways that are a lot more responsible. Because...you adjust, you discover, and there are goals that you make in life.

What aspects of Fredy have made him a myth here?

For example, that he is never afraid of talking with people, or of making friends. Also, something else that has made Billabong famous here is that he hooks up with everyone, and also, that he has learned to surf. I think that that has given him more fame than anything else.

Why?

Because even people who have lived here a long time often don't surf. He did not grow up here, but still, he goes surfing. He is not embarrassed to tell the story of where he comes from. He tells everyone his story, and he surfs, and he talks with everyone, and besides that he is always happy. You never see him angry, or grumpy, never....And sometimes, if you argue with him, it could be because he is a bit drunk, but never at other times.

Can you think of a story typical of Billabong?

Something that I like and that's very funny is that, we were always afraid of the big waves when we were learning to surf. And I always told Billabong, Billabong, don't go to Punta Carola, Don't go there. I remember that he had saved up a lot to buy himself a new surfboard, one that no one here had or could have. So, he went to Punta Carola and the waves were immense. He caught a wave and when he fell, the surfboard broke in two! It was only about two days after he'd bought it. And he was so upset, he wanted to cry. But then he repaired the surfboard and sold it to a guy from Guayaquil. And when we were walking in Quito, in the shopping mall, we arrived and saw Billabong's surfboard in the Oakley store. And we went in to ask about it, and the guy there says, yes, this surfboard is very famous because it belongs to a really good surfer from Galápagos, and here all of the stores take turns to exhibit it. Incredible, don't you think?

Yes, I agree, laughing, but thinking, too, how many times and with how many people has Fredy returned to the mainland? I don't remember Fredy ever telling me that he had traveled with Giovanny.

What do you remember about the hotel that Fredy used to have?

Ok, well when he had the hotel, it was something incredible. The hotel was called Hotel San Cristóbal, but it was better known as Billabong's Place [La Casa de

Billabong]. *Why? Because he always welcomed tourists, and backpackers; he always gave a hand to people who couldn't pay for the hotel room, by letting them stay free. And they, what did they do? How did they pay him? They shared their food, or they left him their things when they left. So the place was always full of parties, lots of people...all of his friends hung out there, and damn, it was incredible. We went there to surf, and to watch movies....There was a pool table, and Billabong would always be outside on the patio, sitting at a table, playing cards, and with all of his friends there. We would watch the sunset, and we would stay there at the beach until dark. The hotel had hammocks, too, on trees that are no longer there....It was great.*

Was that when he became famous?

Well, the hotel gave him a little more fame, because he was always helping people there. But what gave him more fame was arriving at a bar, like Iguana, or Scuba, and starting to dance. Because he dances really well. He dances with foreign girls, and it draws a lot of attention.

Do you think that Fredy's past in the jungle influences the way he lives here?

That could be...but I think that his arriving here alone, and having to adapt to the new environment and learn to survive here, influences him more....I have always tried to give him advice to work a bit more, because when you work, this helps you to learn and arrive a bit faster at your goals.

Has Fredy spoken with you about his goals? Do you think he has goals?

Well, the only goal that he has always had in life is to be happy....As a result, in terms of material things, he doesn't have much. I think he also wants to travel.

Giovanny looks up at the trees outside his apartment, then across the street to the beach volleyball game at Playa Mann, and continues:

I think Fredy has learned so many things here. It's that the environment gives you the chance to involve yourself with all types of people, from lots of different cultures. So I think that you learn a little from each of these people and you go seeing how you can apply this in your life.

There are tourist sites all over the world, but Galápagos is unique. The tourists come and become very good friends with the people here....If Billabong were in Quito, in what we call gringolandia,[96] *he would not have options. He would have to work, and he might not have enough time to dedicate himself to his girls, like he does here.*

Giovanny plays a CD for me of Iguanamen, a band from Santa Cruz Island. One song will interest me especially, he says, because in it, Hugo Idrovo, the songwriter and singer, sings about Billabong.

"La Loba"

We arrive at six in the morning
By the blue path from the airport

---

[96] a part of Quito with many shops and restaurants catering to tourists

...
And there Billabong was already,
Casanova surfer, just like in the jungle.
He and Humberto were laughing about all that they had surfed
And the plenty that was to come.
This happiness never goes away
At the Lobería[97]

---

[97] a beach on San Cristóbal near the airport and good surfing spots where sea lions, known as *lobos marinos*, tend to congregate

Reflecting on Two Worlds

Fredy:

I have been on the Galápagos for ten years. And in these ten years, I have changed so much. Like one-hundred-and-eighty degrees, truly. And sometimes, for me, it is something great that I've done. For me, this is my dream that I saw, understand? I don't know, I feel good. Now I have....many things: worries, obligations, I have all that, but I feel good.

Is there anything you miss about the jungle?

Well, there was a bit more freedom there, a little more tranquility, not as much stress and worry.

The good things about the jungle, Fredy says, are that you can enjoy nature and feel like you are king. He also describes how in the jungle, he was friends with all of his siblings equally, and everyone shared everything and was very generous. Whereas outside the jungle, he has found that there is a lot more individualism, less generosity and more inequality.

In the jungle, I had a lot less to do. Here, I have obligations, I have to work to eat, I have to think about what I'm going to do in the future, I have to...do many things. But in the jungle, no. In the jungle, you only walk through the jungle, fish, go and harvest yuca, plantains and corn, and that's all. Here, you have to pay for light, you have to pay for

Internet, you have to pay...so many things...you have to fly in planes...thousands of things like this. Everything is stressful now.

Would you prefer to lead a more simple life?

Yes, I would prefer a more simple life, but I've already...become part of this. There's already the necessity, and obligations, and I have to do this because I'm in the environment where this needs to be done, paying for things and things like that.

Do you think you could return to a life that is more like the life you led in your childhood?

No, I don't think so.

Why not?

Because a lot has changed inside of me. I've changed, maybe three hundred and eighty degrees in my life. And how can I go back? I wouldn't be able to use Internet, or talk on the phone, or have a cell phone. I'm already a modernized Huao.

Fredy and cell phone, Las Tijeretas, 2005

Now you are more modern than savage?

Yes, more modern than savage, exactly.

Do you like life better outside the jungle?

Now, yes, I like it more, because you can do a lot of things. In the jungle, what was there to do? Nothing, nothing.

Where do you have to think more—here, or in the jungle?

Here, definitely. Because here you have a lot of needs. You have to understand a lot of psychology.

Do you bring knowledge from the jungle that helps you in your life here?

Here, no, it doesn't help me at all....It could be that the knowledge that I have here helps me in the jungle, though.

Fredy mentions making cabins, being a guide, and speaking Spanish as examples of new skills he could now apply if he were to return to the jungle.

How does your jungle past affect you?

Before, I was more...timid around people; I couldn't talk about my culture, because they would say, wow, he's indigenous, he's less than we are....

Before, Fredy says, he was more inhibited and distanced. But now, if someone mentions that he is indigenous, Fredy thinks that's great. He's proud of being unique.
Perhaps another sign of Fredy's becoming more comfortable and better adjusted to culture outside the jungle is the near disappearance of the stutter he'd had back in 2001. Fredy, however, says that's just from a lot of talking with people.

This happiness never goes away
At the Lobería....

We visit the Lobería one last time before starting off for the jungle, and I interview Fredy a final time, asking him about how life for his tribe has changed since they became civilized.

"We are starting from zero," Fredy says. The Huaorani were enticed to listen to the missionaries and to the military because these strange outsiders showed them things that were in the outside world, like cars. But how is a Huao going to make the fifteen thousand dollars necessary to buy a car, starting from nothing, not even a conception of working for a living? Fredy says. They just can't.

Don't members of your tribe earn money from tourists now?

Yes, and sometimes someone goes to town to buy things, and returns. Because it is very difficult to leave your land for good and go to the city. In the city, you have to pay for light, water, everything. It's better to stay in the jungle, in your little house, with a candle for light.

How has your family's life changed?

Now they don't go hunting nearly as often. Life is easy now. They eat rice. And they hardly use medicinal plants any more. They have Contax,[98] *aspirin, everything easy. Very few now go and look for plants.*

    Fredy says that his tribe doesn't have television in the jungle yet, but they do have radio. They wear clothes and baseball caps like people in the rest of Ecuador. There is even, Fredy says, a tourist agency in the jungle that organizes tours. He shows me the same picture again of himself and a guy he says is his brother holding an anaconda and standing in front of a small office with a hand-painted sign, the end of which reads "de Gabriel Guallo." Looking this up on the Internet later, I find a picture of the same tourist agency, located near Tena and affiliated with a project called "Allucos de Llanganates" that operates in a

---

[98] similar to Tylenol-brand pain reliever

community called Suma Waisa. The project's website[99] advertises that in addition to rafting, kayaking, and observing jungle plants and animals, the agency offers tourists a chance to observe shamanic rituals and participate in traditional methods of fishing and gold cleaning.

• • •

Missionary Steve Saint, nephew of Rachel Saint and son of Nate Saint, who was speared by the Huaorani in 1956, explained in a 1998 interview:

> "In an uncanny way, I see the Holy Spirit working through the tourism. As the people from the outside have come in, they're not interested in seeing the Huaorani young people standing around to show off their fake Nike tennis shoes. What they're interested in is how the Huarani used to live, but it's only the old people who can show them that….This has raised the value of the old ways in the eyes of the young people, opening a way for the elders to share the Gospel with the next generation."[100]

• • •

---

[99] http://www.uct.edu.ec/info/Proyectos/allucos.htm
[100] Wood, "Fighting Dependency Among 'the Aucas,'" 14.

And do they like it how it is now, more or how it was before?

They like how it is now, because everything is easy. They don't have to go out searching for the plants two days, or one day.

Fredy says that there are very few people who continue to make *chicha* now, because now they can buy packaged juice. "*¿Para qué vas a hacer más?*" Why would you do more?

I say goodbye to the Galápagos for probably the last time, visiting my host mother Mercedes from 2001 and the pelicans along the dock, and Fredy and I head to the airport to wait for our flight to Quito. From Quito, we plan to take a bus to a town called Coca, which seems from Fredy's guidebook like a good base for heading into the jungle.

Amazon Bound

Though he has been on a plane before, Fredy acts like a five-year-old in the seat beside me on the flight over, wondering about the buckle to the seatbelt and how it works. I've noticed this aspect of his personality before, and he himself has spoken of it, too:

Everything is a novelty. Everything is new for me. I'm like a kid, learning all the time, because everything is new for me here.

I am reminded of how Fredy likes to blow bubbles from a wand around his room, sometimes annoying me when I'm trying to continue with an interview. Pointing to the bubbles, he admits that, "Grown ups have no use for this; they'd throw it aside and not think about it." For him, though, it's very interesting.

We land in Quito and I am glad to have Fredy with me so we don't get totally ripped off for the taxi fare to *gringolandia*. I am surprised to see that Fredy seems to be good friends with the owner of our hostel, which works out well because we are able to store our luggage there when we go to the jungle.

For the day and a half that we are in Quito, the culture in the capital city is a bit foreign for both of us, but in different ways: in the Galápagos, walking on and hopping between uneven rocks for about a half hour of the forty-five-minute walk to the surfing spot

Punta Carola, Fredy would go super fast, and I would be out of breath, almost running to keep up with him. He always said he felt part of the *naturaleza*, and couldn't go slowly. On the street, though, I would often walk a bit too fast for him. In Quito, that difference is magnified, as I am at ease in dodging the traffic and crossing the streets, while Fredy seems nervous and paralyzed.

•••

Kane has noted something similar, writing that the stoicism and self-reliance that characterize the Huaorani in the jungle seem to disappear in the town, where they appear shy, deferential, and a little dazed, looking for direction.[101]

•••

Walking through the large, upscale shopping mall in Quito, things that are junky and frivolous to me are fascinating to Fredy, like a display with floating balls and a fortune-telling machine that Fredy insists on dropping coins into.

In the evening, wanting to go out and dance in Quito like we always did in the Galápagos is frustrating because all of the many places to go are sort of hidden, you have to pay a cover charge to get in, and inside, they are all totally jammed, loud, smoky, and reeking of alcohol, with not a lot of room to dance. We play pool somewhere, but it is really

---

[101] Kane, *Savages*, 74.

expensive, and uncomfortable because a lot of guys are staring at us. Are we a strange looking pair?

We stay in Quito for only a day and, after Fredy searching to no avail for the hotel manager woman who owes him his wages, we head off to the jungle.

When we arrive in the jungle city of Coca from Quito after a ten-hour overnight bus ride during which Fredy insists on using change I've given him to buy me a bright yellow, smiling person pillow with arms and legs, we come to a sticky, hot, dirty town. It is dawn, things are just opening, and we have trouble finding a place to stay. We walk over to a brown river, to the side of which stray dogs are milling about and people in dirt-covered, torn clothing are sitting with plantains and squirming, fat, white grubs in baskets, beginning to set up market. Fredy asks men in long, skinny canoes about how long it would take to take us to Yasuní National Park, where Fredy has told me he was born and where we can look for his parents. Twelve hours in the canoe, they say, but the cabins up there are already all booked, so would have to rent a tent and stay in that.

I was hunched over on a bench, exhausted from not sleeping, motion sick, and feeling generally negative about our situation. Why had I trusted Fredy to begin with? It seemed like he was not even interested in trying to find his parents or show me, truly, where he had grown up. No way, I tell Fredy, am I going to sit in a canoe for twelve hours to stay in a tent in the middle of the jungle for two days to be possibly eaten by tigers, snakes and wild boars, when I have a feeling we were not even heading in the right direction to find your family. We go back to the extremely dingy and hot hotel room we'd finally found, where the fan does little except make my beads of sweat evaporate a little faster, and I collapse on the bed, feeling very ill and depressed. In a couple of hours, we go downstairs to a dingy local restaurant, open to rushing motorcycles and full of shady-looking people who are staring openly at me, for breakfast. I ask for *café con leche* with bread and marmalade and eggs, a usual Ecuadorian breakfast that I usually really like at other shops, but here it disgusts me. There is a thick skin on the milk, and chunks of the skin throughout the liquid. The eggs are nearly raw, and make me feel even more ill than I already do. Making my state of mind even worse is that Fredy, as soon as we sit down, leaves, saying "I'll be right back," but by the time I have finished eating, he is still not back. Coca feels very dangerous, more so than Quito or even Guayaquil because there seems like nowhere upscale to retreat to, like a fancy hotel lobby or even a McDonald's. I return to my room to sweat and try to sleep amid the smoke and noise coming in from the single window that looks out on the street. Fredy does not come back for another three hours.

By the time Fredy gets back, I am furious with him and have had enough of the situation. While I recognize that my outlook has changed perhaps alarmingly quickly, too many things have gone downhill and I have no desire to be in the jungle with someone I can't trust and am not getting along with. I tell Fredy that I no longer want to travel with him, because we are not getting along very well and are not having a good time together. I am going to buy a plane ticket back to Quito for either tonight or tomorrow, I tell him, and say that I want to be alone there. In truth, the idea of being by myself in Quito sounds pretty depressing, yet it seems better than feeling so uncomfortable and upset being with Fredy. And, I tell myself, it will give me time to write and transcribe the rest of my interviews before returning to the United States.

Feeling unbearably dirty and nauseated, I go and buy my fifty-dollar plane ticket for the next morning, the earliest they have. I give Fredy forty dollars, which could buy the bus ticket as well as lodging and meals for two days if he is frugal and doesn't waste it on cigarettes and beer.

That afternoon, I wander by myself around Coca, which I've read in Fredy's guidebook was a base for foreign oil companies that came in and have been exploiting oil resources in the area. The town seems pretty bleak, but perhaps not as bleak as I feel inside—alone, guilty about ditching Fredy, my project having come to nothing.

...

Clayton Robarchek writes of "the catastrophic impact of the worldwide industrial megaculture," on the Huaorani, namely, the unquenchable thirst by industrial nations for oil, land, timber, and minerals.[102] Apparently, there has been tremendous pollution caused by oil companies in the northern Oriente, the rainforest region north of the Andes, right around Coca. Daphne Eviatar, for example, says that

---

[102] Robarchek, *Waorani*, 12.

plaintiffs in a twelve-year-long lawsuit against Texaco assert that over about twenty years, Texaco dumped eighteen billion gallons of oil and toxic waste into Ecuador's waterways, causing massive contamination that has led hundreds of Ecuadorians to die of strange cancers.[103] While Ecuador depends on oil for more than half of its revenues, under Ecuadorian law, writes Kane, the Huaorani have no control over oil production and no share in these profits. For a bit of perspective, Kane notes that the Texaco pipeline dumped one and a half times as much oil into the Oriente as the Exxon Valdez spilled off the coast of Alaska.[104]

...

Later that evening, when Fredy comes back to the room to get his things before leaving for Quito on the bus, we are both really upset. I tell Fredy how sad I am, but he assures me that he feels worse than I do. "I feel like garbage," Fredy says, and starts to cry. Fredy talks about the special connection that he has felt between us, and tells me he doesn't understand how I could just want to abandon him and not see him again.

Seeing Fredy's tears, I am relieved to realize that there *is* some depth to our relationship. He's not totally untrustworthy, I tell myself, and definitely not ill-meaning. I wasn't totally crazy to have come here with him after all. "I ran into a cousin of mine in the street," Fredy goes on, "and he has invited us to his

---

[103] Eviatar, "The High Cost of Oil."
[104] Kane, *Savages*, 5–6, 18.

house in the jungle. What a shame that we can't go." His cousin Fausto and his wife, Fredy explains, are this very minute right across the street at a bar, and Fredy has told them that he'll be right back. I stop and consider. Even though it would mean losing our plane and bus tickets, I feel that going across the street with Fredy is the right thing to do—isn't this, after all, what we have come to the jungle for, to meet some of Fredy's family and experience their way of life? I pack up my things and we head across the street to meet Fausto and his wife.

TASTING *CHICHA*

After a half-hour taxi ride, we arrive at the spot in the road closest to Fausto's mother's place. It is completely dark, so I have to just hope that I am not going to step on a snake. Fredy asks, surprised, don't they have lights? And they respond that they did for a little while, but that the power has been out for about two weeks. Fredy is the only one who seems bothered by this. I realize that the house is elevated: I feel plank wooden stairs under my feet, leading to an upstairs area largely open to the outside air, where we sit down on a bench and Fausto begins to explain to me that I am welcome, and that the next day we will share many things, talk. He will share with me, he says, I will share with him, and he will take me to meet a shaman, and it will be very nice. While Fausto is trying to talk, Fredy interjects loud, annoying, insensitive comments, and I feel like telling him to be quiet but I know that as the guest, that is not my place.

Inside of Fausto's jungle home

Fausto and his wife offer us their bed, with sheets and a mosquito net, while they sleep on the floor with the children. Fredy snores so loudly, I have a lot of trouble sleeping, and my pushing him in different positions does not quiet the noise. In the pitch darkness, I do not want to go out in the jungle by myself, so I hold in my urine for the night. In the morning, though, I really have to go, and I ask Fredy if there is somewhere to go to the bathroom. He stands and pees off the side of the platform floor, but he says he really doesn't know where I should go, and he asks Fausto's young daughter, about three years old, if she can show me how to go to the bathroom here. "There is no bathroom." she tells him, and he says, "Show her, show her how." So I follow the three-year-old down a path and then into the trees. Here, she says, pointing to a log on the ground. Here? I say? Uh huh, she nods. The solids, too? I try to ask. Uh huh. As she stands watching, I pull down my pants and sit precariously on the log, with most of my behind sticking out in back. I wonder if this is what I am expected to do. The girl watches me, curious and silent. When I am done, she perches herself on the log, squatting but with her feet on top of the log, and does her business that way. We leave, and I am so grateful for her having led me somewhere I could relieve myself!

Being at Fausto's house, even though it is much more modern than the uncontacted tribal houses Fredy described, I can put a picture to some of the things Fredy has told me about life in the jungle. I try the Huaorani "fountain of life," *chicha de yuca*, for instance, and see the wooden trough where the white liquid is left to ferment. The drink has a sour taste, and a consistency of glue mixed with water, with small chunks of the starchy yuca floating in it. I only manage to swallow a few sips.

The author tasting *chicha de yuca*

While Fredy sleeps in, I ask Fausto and his wife questions about their lifestyle, and hear that they do eat snakes, monkeys, and other animals, like Fredy has said. Fausto knows how to do some shamanistic things and is learning more. He shows me the marks on his hands from handling the hot charcoal that he passes over people's bodies to heal them. Fausto and his wife have two small children, who they say attend a school that either missionaries or the government have set up for their village. But it's hard, Fausto says, because if the children go to school, it means families have to stay in one place and can't roam around the jungle to hunt as they once did. The children learn to read and write in Spanish, but they do not learn the ways of the jungle, like how to find and recognize medicinal plants. Actually, Fausto's wife is from the Quechua tribe—it seems that Huaorani men often marry Quechua women because they find them more beautiful.

• • •

Laura Rival notes that oil companies are now trying to control the Huaorani like the missionaries once did, creating programs for modernization that, according to Rival, "are undermining what constitutes the core of Huaorani culture: their unique relationship to the forest and their hunting-gathering way of life."[105] Because of schools, for instance, Rival notes that Huaorani parents "are forced to become sedentary agriculturalists, and to produce food for children who are no longer autonomous food producers...."[106]

I ask Fausto what the effect of the missionaries has been on him and his family. Have they adopted the Christian faith? No, Fausto says, smiling maybe conspiratorially. In my heart I haven't changed my beliefs. We just take what they give us, and that's it.

Missionary Stephen E. Saint believes that Christianity is responsible for a large decline in killing among the Huaorani and the tribe's nearly tripling its population in the years since contact with the missionaries began. Saint, who is featured in the somewhat sensationalist film *End of the Spear*, is the

---
[105] Rival, *Trekking Through History*, xvi.
[106] Rival, *Trekking Through History*, 172.

son of Nate Saint, who was speared by the Huaorani in 1956. He currently lives with the Huaorani and writes that "...some of the very men who speared my father have become substitute grandfathers to my children."[107] According to Saint, "...there is unmistakable evidence among certain Huaorani Christians today of a strong desire not only to follow Christ but to share the gospel with others (self-propagation)."[108] Yet, he admits that, "The Huaorani have become dependent on outsiders—specially [sic] North American Christians—for education, for medical and dental services, and for radio communications to relay information between their many villages." Saint explains that some of this dependency was created by oil companies and government agencies. "Unlike oil companies, however," he writes, "the church has a great deal to lose from creating dependency. While most missionaries would not consciously foster dependency, I believe the Devil deceives us into creating this state by prompting us to mix into our legitimate desire to help others a small measure of pride and a dose of cultural arrogance."[109]

• • •

When Fredy gets up, we all walk down to the river, where Fausto demonstrates how he fishes with a net, and his wife begins to wash clothes. I dig up some yuca from their *chacra*, sample some typical

---

[107] Saint, "The Unfinished Mission to the 'Aucas.'"
[108] Saint, "The Unfinished Mission to the 'Aucas.'"
[109] ibid.

jungle fruits that I've never seen before, and watch the family point out a "real" Huaorani man to me—he doesn't wear clothes, just a string around his waist, they exclaim, laughing. I only catch his backside as he darts up the side of the riverbank.

Fausto's family members themselves wear worn-out American-style clothing: T-shirts, pants, shorts, and baseball caps. Their house consists of two rooms—one for cooking and eating, and the other for sleeping. There is no table, but wooden benches built into the wall of the eating room. The most striking thing to me about their house is its lack of walls to the outside—the temperature really must not vary much, I think, if it is comfortable to have the outside temperature be the same as the inside temperature all of the time. The most important distinction between outside and inside their house seems to be the lack of jungle animals inside—which is accomplished, I suppose, by having the house raised up to second-story level.

Fausto showing the author how to pick yuca

Sitting on some logs among pecking chickens underneath his raised house, I interview Fausto but my equipment fails and I lose the recording. Fausto tells me that yes, he knew Fredy as a child, but doesn't have anything specific to say when I ask him what Fredy was like back then. He says that he himself attended school as a child, that's how he learned Spanish, which does not make sense to me if Fredy was telling the truth about not having had any contact with civilization as a child. After all, wouldn't Fredy have attended school or have had at least some contact with missionaries if his cousin, whom he spent time with, did?

...

Joe Kane, who traveled with a Huaorani man named Enqueri to conduct a census among the tribe, describes one group of Huaorani known as the ridge group who lived downriver from the missionary Protectorate area and may have managed to evade most missionary influence. He writes:

> "While it is probably true that no Huaorani have escaped at least some influence by the missionaries—among even the most remote clans, one occasionally spots a Maidenform bra—contact with the ridge group had been minimal, and our proposed trek caused Enqueri no small anxiety....Visitation rights among the Huaorani are determined by a complex system of familial ties, and anyone lacking them, even a Huao, is considered an enemy."[110]

...

Fausto seems ready to bring me around to meet a shaman and show me other things, but I am feeling sad, troubled by my broken minidisc player and the lost interviews, hungry, and fatigued. Fredy does not seem to be doing well either and asks if I want to leave and go to Tena for a few days, take day trips to see some jungle animals, maybe go rafting. A hotel does sound good to me, and we decide to leave as soon as possible.

Waiting for a bus to Tena that would pass by the newly constructed road below, we sit with Fausto, his mother, and his brother, wife, and children at his mother's home. Offering us *chicha*, *tío* just lounging in the hammock, no one with anything pressing to do, all afternoon to just sit and talk. Like at Fausto's, there

---

[110] Kane, *Savages*, 40–41.

is a low wooden bench along the wall, but here there are also chairs and a table, which holds an assortment of coloring books, markers, and notebooks that the *abuela* says they got for free from the oil company in exchange for their community having the company's bridge in the area.

•••

According to Kane, the Ecuadorian government now lets the oil company Maxus be in control of Huaorani health and education.[111] Eviatar writes that Huaorani communities that made deals with oil companies received motors for their canoes, soccer balls, chainsaws to build houses, and, in at least one case, a school. Some of these communities, Kane writes, "can now call the oil companies for emergency transportation and modern healthcare, which is otherwise nonexistent in the rainforest."[112]

•••

Fredy shows the family pictures from the Galápagos and of himself surfing, and tells them that he may be getting married to a Swiss girl soon. They don't show any particular reaction. I ask the family the same questions I've been asking everyone I encounter who experienced jungle life before the influence of the missionaries and oil companies became so strong: how is your life different now? Do you like things better now, or the way they were

---

[111] Kane, *Savages*, 161.
[112] Eviatar, "The High Cost of Oil."

before? To which I don't get clear answers, except that their food has changed a lot: now they buy and eat rice and sugar, so their diet is less dependent on animal prey. Wild animals, of course, have become scarcer anyway with the coming of "civilization."

⋯

Laura Rival writes that the Huaorani have accepted modern food like rice, powdered milk, sugar, and oats, in order to become modern and civilized, which to them means becoming "whiter, fatter, and softer."[113] Seeing him next to Fausto, I tease Fredy that he has become fatter and softer than his cousin, by living more inside of civilization as he does in the Galápagos.

⋯

After several hours, we hear a bus coming and run down to the road to catch it. Luckily, it is going to Tena, and we hop on. As I stare out the window at all the jungle foliage, wondering about the lifestyles and secrets that it holds, I hear Fredy strike up a conversation with a woman sitting across from us, asking her where she is from and how many children she has. The woman turns to me and asks my age. When I say twenty-four, she says in comparison that she had had five children by the time she was twenty-four. Yes, I think, I know that this is not my world. There is no question that I am an outsider to the ways of the jungle and rural Ecuador.

---

[113] Rival, *Trekking Through History*, 164.

Adventures in Tena

Fredy and I arrive some hours later in the town of Tena, which in contrast to Coca seems extremely clean and friendly. Fredy has been to Tena before with a couple of his past girlfriends, he says, and by the way he is remembered and welcomed by the manager of the hostel where we are staying, it seems like since the time he lived here fresh out of the jungle he has been back to this town more than once. In our room, Fredy is mesmerized by watching shows on the National Geographic Channel on television. It seems strange—I have come all the way to Ecuador to find some "real," "adventurous," or "native" stories and information, which is what National Geographic tends to cover, and Fredy, my subject, is mesmerized by the same things that he himself represents for me!

In Tena, I talk more with Fredy about the effects of modernity on the Huaorani and he tells me that he thinks that being in contact with civilization has brought new illnesses to the tribe and hurt them overall medically, since now people are forgetting the traditional herbal remedies and sometimes cannot pay for the drugs they need.

> "Since the white people arrived, unknown illnesses have come to the Huaorani. For these new illnesses we do not have the appropriate medicines. Before, it wasn't like

that: each sickness had its corresponding herb and medicine."[114]

—Huepe, one of Lino Tagliani's Huaorani informants

...

Fredy's general savoir-faire shines in Tena, where he has no problem convincing taxi drivers to drive us around to various places and wait for us as we go to a truck repair shop, for instance, and rent inner tubes. In the cabs, Fredy is always talking, joking with the *taxista* and making him feel comfortable and amused. One afternoon, after picking up the inner tubes for truck tires, which Fredy negotiates to borrow even without any proper ID to give them as deposit, a taxi drops us off several miles upstream of a river that runs through the town. I am a bit scared to be so exposed in the water, thinking of the possible jungle creatures that might live there, like snakes and piranhas, but rafting does sound fun so I decide to go for it. In the tube, even though I'm probably about the same weight as Fredy, he goes much faster down the river. Left on my own, I get scared and yell at Fredy to wait. It takes about two hours to get down to the town in our tubes, and on the way we pass many people washing their clothes and looking at us curiously. I am grateful to Fredy for arranging this adventure, which luckily ends fairly smoothly, but annoyed at his requests to kiss me when our tubes bump up against one another.

---

[114] Tagliani, *También el Sol Muere*, 186.

Another day, we try to find a jungle wildlife reserve Fredy has heard about in an outlying area, where he can show me some of the jungle animals he grew up with. On a bus in that direction, a young boy and his sister are holding a squirming tan puppy. Fredy, in his normal gregarious fashion, starts talking with them, asking if the puppy eats monkeys and chocolate. They smile and giggle.

Fredy and monkey friend, Tena

The wildlife reserve is hard to get to, so we have a number of adventures on the way. First, we mistakenly get off at an environmental conservation organization called Jatún Sacha, where a lot of *gringos* my age have come to volunteer and live for a few months. As it is pouring rain, we stay there for a few hours, have lunch, and talk with the Americans and

Europeans inside. Normally, I am put off by meeting other Americans when I'm traveling, wanting to seek out a more authentic, non-tourist-oriented experience, but in fact I find it refreshingly confirming of my own culture to talk with these people, whose backgrounds are similar to mine, and share in their eco-consciously vegetarian meal, which Fredy really does not appreciate.

During a break in the rain, Fredy and I head back out to the road, where we wait for a long time but see not even a single vehicle, and then, bored and frustrated, decide to start walking. After about forty minutes, a pickup truck comes, and, seeing us, slows down a little. Fredy nods to the driver, and then calls to me, "Follow me!" as he runs toward the back of the truck and jumps in. With nothing to hold on to as we fly over the many rocks and ditches in the road, I get bumped around quite a bit and come close to falling out a couple of times.

After the truck stops, Fredy negotiates a canoe ride with a Quechua family, and we finally arrive at the wildlife reserve. The thing is, the employees don't let visitors just roam around by themselves—to be allowed in, you have to be with an escorted tour group. We gag, but having no other option, we go in with a group of old, overweight European tourists who have come on a special guided tour bus as part of a jungle travel package. As they chatter, ooh, and ahh over the caged parrots the guide is pointing out, Fredy signals to me and we escape the group and run off on our own, where we freely look at small tigers, toucans, and wild boars that Fredy tells me stories about—that is, until we hear a couple of employees looking for us, and literally have to run.

Quechua woman navigating us on jungle river

On the way back to Tena, I take advantage of being caught in the rain with a local woman and ask how she feels about the changes coming in. Well, it would be fine, she says—the road is a much faster way to town than the river—if only the animals for hunting did not run away. The roads, the people come in, and now it is hard to find something to eat.

•••

In the words of Kane's Huaorani informant Quemperi, "A road means bad hunting. Game won't cross it. Colonists will come and cut down the forest and kill the animals." Kane explains, "A road, in other words, meant hunger. It meant the end of abundance, and the end of the self-reliance and interdependence the Huaorani value above all else."[115]

---

[115] Kane, *Savages*, 36.

...

    In a karaoke bar back in Tena, a girl looking about seventeen enters and comes up to Fredy, kissing him on the cheek and greeting him warmly, looking somewhat amused. She is his niece, she tells me, the daughter of one of his sisters. Apparently Fredy's sister lives in the area of Tena, and the girl is working at someone's house in the city, cleaning. I ask the niece if she knows where Fredy's parents are living, and she says yes, and tells us the name, which I assume that Fredy remembers, but when I ask him later he says he forgot.

    After the girl leaves, I ask Fredy how she knows him, or knows what he looks like. He says he doesn't know, that he doesn't remember ever meeting her, but that last time he was in Tena, he did send some pictures of himself in the Galápagos along with someone who knew his family to share them with his family, so perhaps she recognizes him from there.

    I ask Fredy if he wants to go and visit his sister, and he responds that he wouldn't know how to find where she lives. Why don't you ask your niece, I ask. Fredy's entire story begins to sound fishy to me, as if this whole time Fredy has not been telling me the truth about his family and his past.

    Fredy's response also seems to indicate that he really does not want to see his family. When I question him about this, he tells me that it is just that he doesn't feel he can visit his family with me, since they aren't living in an area that usually receives tourists. He could go somewhere as my guide, but to go just to visit the family, that would only work if I were going to be his wife. And in that case, he says, his family would give me several tests, like making sure I am able to prepare the *chicha de yuca*, before accepting me. It seems like Fredy is implying that his family is not at all pleased that he has changed so much by leaving them and their way of life.

•••

Our jungle week is almost over and it's time for us to head back to Quito where I'll then continue on to Guayaquil to catch my flight back to New York. On the bus from Tena to Quito, as I press tightly to myself, feeling irritated and trying to ward off motion sickness, Fredy talks in English with a couple of German tourists, telling them how he knows people from various parts of Germany, that he is a salsa teacher and a bartender. Oh yeah? they ask, clearly hooked by Fredy's charm. What nationality drinks the most? Well, Fredy starts, the Swiss drink the most X, the British the most Y… he spreads smiles all around.

Crêpe Talk

> "It requires only a change in accent to see continuities and not just differences between the posited unities of primitive cultures and the analytic modes of modern life."[116]
> —Marianna Torgovnick, *Primitive Passions*

Back in Quito the second time, it is awkward being with Fredy because I am excited to go to touristy places to eat, remembering amazing food I'd had in *gringolandia* with the other WorldTeach volunteers in 2001, but Fredy is less than impressed. The food in the restaurants geared toward tourists is not only at least three or four times more expensive than in the restaurants for locals, it is also largely distasteful to Fredy. Presented with a menu, Fredy looks at all the choices, confused and unhappy. He says he cannot understand why anyone would want to eat a salad—it's just leaves. Pizza, too, he does not like. Or maybe, he says, it's all right as a snack. When the bill comes and it's over twenty dollars, I feel awkward as Fredy watches me take out my credit card and sign for it as though it's nothing. If I can afford to pay twenty dollars for a meal for just the two of us, I realize, it must have looked really stingy to Fredy the way I was being frugal in my approach to spending in general over the course of the trip.

---

[116] Torgovnick, *Primitive Passions*, 211.

On my last night in Ecuador, we eat in a crêpe place and have a good talk. Fredy asks me about my plans for the future, and I tell him I am still not sure. That I will be studying documentary radio just for a semester to try it out, and that I applied to be a volunteer with the Peace Corps somewhere in Eastern Europe for two years, so maybe I will do that afterwards. Fredy seems not to understand why I would want to do things that do not make money and that are not heading in a clear direction, career-wise. When I explain that I'm not sure yet what I want to do in terms of a career, he shakes his head.

Fredy thinks that I do not have the same view of the importance of getting ahead in life, of being a professional, because I have never experienced starvation. He says that he would not want his children to be bartenders, or surfers—they should be lawyers, or engineers.

I don't quite understand why Fredy has this view.

Fredy says that he wants to make something of himself, perhaps go to Europe to earn money and then come back and open a surf shop on the Galápagos. He says that it's nearly impossible to save up money by working in Ecuador because of low wages and corruption and lack of organization like I witnessed while I was there—him not having been paid for work he'd done months prior.

At the crêpe place, I explain to Fredy for the first time about my dilemma upon returning to the United States in 2001 and being torn between an image of marrying him and leading a happy, simple life on the Galápagos, and concerns that the

Galápagos did not have the kind of stimulation that I needed, intellectually and artistically and in terms of potential intense, like-minded friends, to sustain me. Fredy seems flattered that I had thought about marrying him, and asks me how I feel about it now. For some reason, the idea does not completely turn me off, and we agree that if in a few years, neither of us is married, we will consider marrying one another.

Fredy and the author on their last evening together, 2005

When it is time for me to leave for my flight, Fredy and I have breakfast at the airport. In a fairly awkward moment, Fredy tells me that he's spent all the money I gave him in Coca and asks me if I can give him some money so he can afford to stay somewhere before his flight back to the Galápagos. I am annoyed that he's spent the money I gave him so quickly, but at the same time annoyed at myself for not feeling more generous toward Fredy. Hasn't he just spent every minute of the past three weeks with me, being my friend and companion and being open to my pursuing my documentary project? I go to the

ATM and get out fifty dollars for him, but the whole thing is uncomfortable. Fredy giving me things that I want and yet at the same time developing an unhealthy dependency on me. Not at all unlike, perhaps, the way the Huaorani became dependent on missionaries and other outsiders.

Fredy and I say goodbye and I feel sad and relieved at once. Maybe I will never see Fredy again. Do I want to see Fredy again? Perhaps I have already learned from him all that I can, we have learned from one another all that we can, and it is time to move on.

On my flight back to New York on the newly formed, nearly entirely Ecuadorian-cliented airline Lan Ecuador, it was apparent that even Ecuadorians wealthy enough to fly to the United States have significant cultural differences between airplane travelers from the United States. When the plane landed, the passengers all clapped and cheered—flying was novel and exciting, and they were truly appreciative for landing safely—how wonderful! Whereas for other seasoned travelers from the north and myself, landing is no big deal. Landing is time to start worrying about getting our luggage and meeting our schedules. We think of the burdens of traveling, rather than looking at things as miraculous. Plus, for me, at least, New York is not the land of wonder and opportunity that it might be for people from Ecuador. In fact, bright lights, expensive clothing, and hustle and bustle are just the things that part of me wants to escape. Still, the cheering made me smile, and that energy and simplicity of reaction was definitely something that I want to be a part of and bring with me in my life wherever I go.

DIGGING UP DIRT

Before I left Ecuador, I asked Fredy to give me the e-mail addresses of some of his past girlfriends so I could contact them in the hopes that they could give me more information about Fredy. Overall, their comments matched well with my own experience of being with and observing Fredy. Two, though, said that they actually did meet Fredy's parents, as well as two of his brothers. This made me feel even less trusting of Fredy, for he must have known where his family was living all along and just did not want to take me there.

Janet Tilempi,[117] one of Fredy's ex-girlfriends, wrote me to say that she went to visit Fredy's family with him, and that they were living in a village called Fatima, outside Puyo. She describes Fatima as "a typical poor Ecuadorian village [with] the houses all built along a road." She met Fredy's brothers Marco and Washington, but she says they never talked about the past. She writes, "When you see how they live you can understand how proud Fredy is about his life in Galápagos. Once he was really drunk in Santa Cruz and was starting to get really melancholy and told me stuff about going back to live in the jungle, because he was missing his family and his roots in the rainforest, but when you see where they live—he would never want to go back." Janet says that she also met one of Fredy's sisters close to Misahualli, and describes how the whole family was watching TV when she and

---

[117] name changed to protect privacy

Fredy arrived and neither Fredy's sister nor his brothers seemed very excited about seeing him.

Janet is twenty-nine and from Switzerland. She met Fredy in February 2004 on Santa Cruz Island where he was taking the scuba diving certification course with Victor that he never finished. Fredy told Janet a lot about Eliane, his Swiss girlfriend who she thinks has been Fredy's only big love. After a night of drinking, "we ended up in bed together and then were a couple for two weeks. We were pretending that it's just for sex..." but she ended up going back to Ecuador to travel and met up with Fredy again in January of 2005 in Quito, when she traveled all over Ecuador for two months with him and Madeline.

Janet: "What I really, really like about Fredy is the easy way he sees the world. He can make you laugh, tell great stories, make you feel like his number one. Both times it was like that. When you're together with him, the world is so ok. But if you're gone he will never tell you the truth about other girls." (For instance, Fredy never told Janet I was coming again.) "I think he's not used to being friends with women. There are girlfriends, maybe some of them he really loves, and of course it's also an easy way to get money." She says she knows that various girls send him money to pay for his room and for diving courses.

Janet continues, "I think Fredy is pretty intelligent, but lazy. He could do a lot with his life, but it's easier to go surfing and be with girls." She writes that he has a natural skill as a motivator—when the two of them traveled together, for instance, Fredy would sometimes organize volleyball games with whoever was around. Everyone got to have fun, and he got to be the boss.

...

According to Kane, the Huaorani think that lying in a hammock doing next to nothing is the highest state of grace a human can achieve. Until the arrival of the missionaries, the Huaorani had no word for or concept of laziness.[118]

similarities

...

Janet also thinks Fredy is lonesome: "I always had the impression with his friends he has to pretend to be cool, they talk about girls, girls, girls, surfing, soccer...but I never heard them talking about feelings."

Anne Eljkman,[119] from Holland, is currently working in Guatemala City as a capacity builder, working with young people in the prevention of youth gangs. She writes that in early 2004, she met Billabong during a trip to Ecuador to teach English at several primary schools in the jungle. "I planned a short trip to the Galápagos," she writes, "but after I met Fredy I spent much more time over there with him. We danced together on the night we met. I never could dance salsa, but with Fredy it went so easy. His strange laugh touched me....He showed me the most beautiful places of the islands and we had a short

---

[118] Kane, *Savages*, 136.
[119] name changed to protect privacy

romance. I was really touched by his story: he was always waiting for girls to come back!" "Sometimes he was so mature and sometimes he was like a little boy and cried. He told me that he was on a holiday to the coast with his family one day, when he saw a plane. He was determined to fly with it, so he took the first plane to Galápagos (the cheapest flight) and he never came back...in love with the islands. He taught me to enjoy life and take it as it is."

> "For me," Anne writes, "it is a paradise over there...and I am still spending a lot of time dreaming about it and hoping to end up there one time. With him. Although I know that he has a lot of girlfriends... (I actually wrote sometimes with another ex-girlfriend of his). But when I have the money I want to go there to live the life easy and relaxing. Not just for him of course...but the environment over there it's 'precioso'! And the culture is great, there is almost no crime and hate, and right now I am living in a violent and dangerous culture in Guatemala. So, the daydreaming about Billabong and 'his' islands get me through it! I think he has this effect on a lot of girls who are getting out of their lives for a while to travel...but they always leave again, and the 'game' goes on for him to win another blond girl...." (e-mail Oct. 05)

While I was in the Galápagos in 2005, Fredy's friends kept bringing up a girl named Madeline, whom they said Fredy was engaged to marry. When I asked Fredy about Madeline, he said yes, Madeline did want to get married, but he was not sure if he did. She was planning to come back to the Galápagos in a couple of months to marry him, though!

Fredy explained that he likes to live one day at a time. "I might marry her or I might not; it depends," he told me. I felt bad for Madeline, knowing that Fredy was not responsible enough to make a commitment to her or fully reveal to her how many other girls might be in his life. Here he was, engaged to be married, and making moves to seduce me!

Madeline wrote to me several months after I left Ecuador:

> "The last six months I was together with him. Our plan was to get married. But after talking a lot, we thought it was better to wait until I finish my university. I know you asked him many times what happened with me and if I was in Galápagos. I don't know what he told you about me, but probably you didn't know I was together with him all this time.
>
> I flew back to Holland last Friday and we said goodbye in Quito. I feel so sad right now, because I really love him and he loves me too. But the problem is I am not the only one. When you are together with him he can give you the feeling that you are the only one. But as soon as you are gone, you don't know what happens in Galápagos. And to all the girls he was with

he writes things like *"te extraño, te amo por siempre, quiero estar contigo por siempre, quiero verte otra vez."* And that is also one of the reasons why I don't want to get married with him yet. I don't know if he is ready to have a serious relationship and just be with one girl. I know he loves me and I will definitely go back to Galápagos again. And we will see what the future brings!!!

I met him the end of November 2004 while I worked as a volunteer in San Cristóbal. We had a lot of fun together and than he told me he was going to travel with a girl from Switzerland, Janet. And he wanted [me to go] travel with them. After thinking a lot I thought ok why not!!! We traveled two months together in Ecuador and we had such a great time. Janet and I really liked each other and we are still in contact. After that Billabong and I traveled in Peru. And we were five months together. Everything passed so fast and I really fell in love with him.

Billabong is a great person with a good heart. He is different than the other boys I met in Galápagos. He is very open and he has so much energy. Always busy with everything. He can talk with everybody, young or old, rich or poor. And he can tell great stories and he is so funny. When I was a little angry about something,

I think ten minutes later I already was laughing about his jokes.

I also think he is really intelligent. Like he always says, "I have a solution for everything." And that's true. When I think something is not possible, he has a solution. There is nothing he can't fix. And I love to see him dance!!

But on the other side, like I already said, it's difficult for him to be honest. When it's about other girls you never know if he is saying the truth. It was for me really hard when I knew you were together with him. But I hope you enjoyed the time together.

And another problem is the alcohol, but that's a problem in whole Galápagos. The people drink too much. When they buy a bottle of vodka, it has to be empty the same night.

He can be really lazy. When he has some money he doesn't work anymore and goes surfing all day.

We visited his family in Puyo and went hiking with them in the rainforest
But his family didn't show a lot of e~
It looked like they didn't care t.
see him again. But maybe tha\
they have twelve children, I don't \

He also doesn't like to sleep in the dark. He always wants the light or the television on. And he moves a lot in his sleep. He always tells me he was dreaming about being in the rainforest and being in the war. I think he has a kind of trauma of the war. On his back he has a big scar, a punishment in the army."

In another e-mail, in response to some of my questions, Madeline writes:

"Hey Carla!!

Well about Billabong's family, they live in the little village Fatima close to Puyo. I've met his parents, some brothers, uncle and cousin, and his grandmother. And they don't live a traditional lifestyle. They only go fishing, but I believe that's it. They have a big garden where they have all kinds of fruits and vegetables. They wear normal clothes and live like poor farmers, but no traditional *indigena* rituals.

About the missionaries I don't know anything, I have no idea when they contacted the tribe. And the story that he had been a cannibal, to be honest I don't believe it. Maybe that a long time ago his ancestors were cannibals. I don't know the habits of the Huaorani, but that's possible.

But I don't believe Billabong ate human meat.

I know he went to school in Fatima (primary education or how you call it), but I don't know how old he was when they moved to Fatima.

When I met him he also told me that he came from the rainforest and that his family still lived in the rainforest among the snakes and the jaguars. But they just live in a village close to Puyo. But that's Billabong, he likes to make stories more exciting than they really are.

I wish you good luck in Azerbaijan and enjoy your time there. Have fun!!!!!

Madeline"

Tying the Vines

> "Often, Westerners seem like Adam and Eve banished from the Eden of the primitive, convinced that some ecstatic primal emotions have been lost, almost as a penalty for being Western. Yet...what is now sought in the primitive is really a reflection or projection of something that could also be found in the West at many different times, in many different forms—and can even be found today."[120]
> —Marianna Torgovnick, *Primitive Passions*

Fredy and I met on the Galápagos—an in-between point. He started from the primitive, going in the direction of development and modernization, while I started from the modernized, and in a sense have been going backwards. I think we are both searching for the same thing, however: the ideal balance for each of us to be able to find happiness.

Despite our dissimilar pasts, Fredy and I share a connection in our energies that our diverse backgrounds make all the more significant. Thinking seriously about it now, however, I know that I would not want to live with or be in a romantic relationship with Fredy. For though he is truly generous and good-hearted, much of our connection from 2001 has been lost. For one thing, I am no longer in need of his guidance in getting in touch with my own physicality

---

[120] Torgovnick, *Primitive Passions*, 210.

and flow. Intellectual connection is lacking from our relationship, as is trust on some levels. (Although perhaps not on the most fundamental ones.) If I were to want to raise a child on my own or with a female partner, however, I cannot think of anyone whose blood I would rather combine with mine.

Andrew Sinclair mentions that with books like Carson's *Silent Spring*, about the dangers of pesticide pollution, there is a modern idea of wanting to return to what is green or savage. But in his estimation, there is "limited hope of returning a materialistic civilization back to the lesser rewards of living nearer to nature."[121] Sinclair's view is that primitivism demands simplicity, yet simplicity is no longer possible. I don't know why that should be the case. I know that my own life has benefited, become more satisfying, from adopting a less frenetic pace and consuming a smaller amount of the world's resources. As I write this, in fact, I am preparing to head off to a less modernized area of the world yet again, to participate in a pace of life that I'm sure will be a lot slower than the one I grew up with and hopefully to continue to learn from a more simple mode of existence.

How much of Fredy's story is true? Well, I believe his family is Huaorani, and that he has knowledge of the jungle. Clearly, however, he had some contact with civilization in his childhood. Could Fredy's story about running away from his tribe be true? Laura Rival writes of two groups of Huaorani, the Tagaeri and the Taromenani, who are still "uncontacted" and refuse to become civilized. Could

---

[121] Sinclair, *The Naked Savage*, 172.

Fredy's family have been from one of those groups? Rival says that civilized Huaorani have boasted to her that they will try to pacify the Tagaeri, telling her that if they get them to eat rice and sugar, then they'll surely become tame and gentle.[122] Randy Smith, too, has written of these two groups who have refused contact with the outside world. The Tagaeri, he says, are also known as the Patas Coloradas, the Patas Rojas, or the Pies Rojos, meaning red feet, because they paint their feet red with achiote when at war.[123]

In 2001, after first meeting Fredy, I definitely ascribed to the philosophy of primitivism, which Marianna Torgovnick describes as "the utopian desire to go back and recover irreducible features of the psyche, body, land, and community—to reinhabit core experiences."[124] Now, after seeing how Fredy misled me about his life story, I have a newfound appreciation of reason, fact, truth, and analysis. Is Fredy part of the "real" primitiveness as I had hoped and imagined? Probably not. He is, however, a lot closer to the primitive in his background than I am.

Perhaps my view of primitive culture is rosier than it should be, but I still strongly believe that modern civilization has a lot to learn from more simple ways of life. After all, as I know first-hand, Western symbols of accomplishment like getting into Harvard are not at all necessarily tickets to happiness.

I thought Fredy had answers for how to live. He does have insights, but I've learned to trust myself

---

[122] Rival, "Ecuador."

[123] Smith, *Crisis Under the Canopy*.

[124] Torgovnick, *Primitive Passions*, 5.

more and not idealize others so much. While I am still searching for a balance between the simple and the complex and am not sure where I will end up, thanks to Fredy, I have a better understanding of energy, human connectedness, and different ways of life that will no doubt help me in my quest.

Currently, I am across the world in the Caucasus country of Azerbaijan, serving as a Peace Corps Volunteer in a small village. On our satellite television last night, I saw the same rocks, iguanas, and sea lions where Fredy surfs—a feature on the Galápagos. While I know now that there is no chance of my marrying Fredy and I have little desire to return to the islands, I feel good knowing that Fredy is in the world, surfing, laughing, riding waves as they come, and helping others to enjoy and do the same.

Fredy surfing, 2001

Epilogue

**Instant Messenger Chat via Internet
(Translated from Spanish)
February 5, 2006
Portland, Maine, USA–Quito, Ecuador**

Hi Fredy

```
Hiiiii
```

What's up? Where are you, in Quito?

```
well.
```

how is it going with your project

```
yes in quito
for a few days
more or less
```

fine…

```
I'm going surfing.
I invite you let's go
```

with friends from other countries?
no, *querido*, I can't.
I'm very far away

```
maybe with friends from quito
```

there's a movie that came out
about the Huaorani

there's also a surfing competition

and the incident in 1956
it's called End of the Spear

I have to participate
oh, yes?

yes, I have several questions for you

ok, go ahead

because now I know more about your tribe
what are your parents' names?

Rafael shicuany

Rafael is the name of your father?
It seems like a Spanish name

no, indigenous

but this is real
but before the civilization

?

ayaaaaa

what?

yutury
which means

like the most capable bird
in the jungle
and my mother nina which means fire

Do you know that Dayuma, then?

when I was little
but now
she's the current boss
like the president
of that whole region

but now does your family continue to live in the Protectorate?

no

since when did your family live in the protectorate? because I thought it was formed in the 60s

who formed in the 60s
I don't understand

the missionaries created the Protectorate in the 1960s and they brought a lot of huaoranis to live there

yes
of course
it was to help the mission

and your family went to live there during that time? in the 60s?

yes of course.

so you had contact with missionaries all your life then, right?

do you know a huaorani man named Mincaye? because he shows up a lot in the movies that came out about your tribe here.

```
no
because you can't know
everybody.
because we didn't all live close by
```

but he did live in the protectorate, and was involved in the incident in the Curaray River in 1956

```
we used to walk
through that whole zone
```

you didn't live very close to where Dayuma lived with Rachel Saint, and where they had put up the radios?

```
I didn't live near there
sometimes you had to travel for a day by
canoe
```

look…what I don't understand is: if there was contact with the missionaries in 1956 and your family lived in the region of the Protectorate, how could your family have escaped contact with civilization during your childhood? because before you told me that your tribe hadn't been contacted before you were around 10 or 11.
do you remember the names of other people who lived with you during your childhood?

```
those people are already dead
```

that's fine, but do your remember any of their names?

```
patary
dandy
liona
```

and your brothers—you showed me someone in a photo—what are their names?
how did those people die?

```
like sicknesses like from crossing the rivers
from anacondas
and others by tigers
the jungle is not very safe you know
there are all the dangers
```

from my studies, there was no incident with missionaries during your lifetime—only in 1956. you were telling me about what happened before you were born, right?

```
yes
it was many years ago
```

were the people who killed the missionaries from your family or community? or from another one?

```
it's the same one, from another section or place
```

did you grow up eating rice?

```
no
in those times there was no rice
```

I didn't understand that—they weren't from your family?
but they did have contact with the bible and things like that?

```
members of the community
but I tell you that I haven't spoken much about this
you know these stories are little told
```

do any members of your family live in the protectorate now?

```
yes of course
it's our family that of dayuma
```

what?

```
through my grandmother
```

your grandmother is a sister of dayuma?

```
they're cousins or something like that
```

and your grandmother lives in the protectorate?
what's your grandmother's name?

```
cuji
```

how much contact did your family have with the missionaries during your childhood?

```
not much
```

can you explain that a little for me—what happened? the missionaries would visit you sometimes, or what?

```
for my tribe
yes of course after the incident
they almost had access
but more to teach
about the bible
because we had our own god
```

and some missionaries lived in your community?

yes

were they catholic, or protestant?
from Ecuador, or the united states?

```
they were of the catholic
religion
```

I don't understand. your family lived within the protectorate, but separate from the community where Dayuma lived with Rachel Saint (a big, white, and fat woman)?
missionaries lived in your community, but you didn't eat rice?
how did it work?

```
I didn't like it
I didn't want to change
my favorite food
fish
and wild animals
but the rice was only for them
afterwards yes
because then they brought more to give
```

I've read that life inside the protectorate was very sedentary for the huaorani was your family sedentary because it lived inside that region with the missionaries?

```
what is sedentary
```

that it didn't move—it stayed in one spot, in one village

```
yes it moved
```

Toñampare—this is the name of the town in the Protectorate. did you live there?

```
for hunting
yes
```

you lived in Toñampare?

```
no
it's small places where you could have ceremonies
or rituals
for the sun god
```

but were you familiar with that town?

```
very little
because when I went
there were some
houses like chozas [thatched huts]
```

ok so now, from your family, who lives in the protectorate?

```
yes
made for protection
by unesco
```

I don't understand. who lives in the protectorate now?
any of your siblings?

```
the other families
```

but not your family?

```
you know that they hunted
and then almost nothing looked at them
```

your family, you're saying? they were hunting animals and that's why they moved around a lot?

```
because in order to hunt that
we had to go farther away from
the town or place
and plant our own crops
```

you don't know the town Quehuere Ono?

```
no
```

okay well...
this is the thing—the missionaries in the Protectorate aren't catholic; they're protestant. They're from the United States.

```
all right and tell me where you are now
```

there were catholic missionaries in other parts....

```
very few I think
truly I don't know
very much
```

Are you sure that you lived inside the Protectorate?
Near where Dayuma lived?
(she lived with people from SIL, a protestant organization)
I'm now in the state of maine
in the north of the country
my classes start tomorrow

about what

documentary radio

how nice
do they pay you

ummm, no. I pay

yes you are lucky like that

what?

it's like a radio volunteer

I worked these past months in an office—very boring
no...a student

how many professions do you want to have
and then you don't know what you want

I think I'm an artist, so I'm not going to have a "profession" exactly, like a doctor or a
pilot

I'm writing songs now

```
really
write one for me and sing
then send it to me
```

maybe....i will try

```
really
```

and you—what happened with the wedding

```
awesome
```

and your plans for Switzerland

```
we're just
going to think
of the opportunities there are
to be happy
```

did Madeline leave, or is she still with you in Ecuador

```
I don't know
I still don't have plans
for a study to be
a pilot
or steward
I have a heart of adventure
to get to know other countries
```

do you have a job in these months?

```
maybe
it's possible I'll work in the same
hotel orca
```

did they pay you finally?

but now as a surfing guide
partly
how long are you going to work at the radio?

four months, not long

if you like it you'll stay longer
and what happened with volunteering
in another country
like you were
applying for

the program is only for 4 months, but if I like it I will make documentaries working on my own, to sell

yes, it's possible that I will do that in june
I'm not sure yet

you can sell in Europe
it would be a good business
with you you never know

haha I'm not sure about that....

you always have plans

well I hope to finish my book in the coming months as well

you want to study sing dance
and everything

maybe I will have to ask more questions, I'm not sure

later

you can ask me more

yes, I like to do many things, not to specialize as much

I'm sure we will be in contact
I'm sure

as you think I should
yes, sounds good
it's so nice to "talk" with you

yes it makes me happy
because I have to think
and I like that
I almost never think
I only act

great—yes, I have a lot of experience in thinking

do you have a telephone number
where I can call you some day if I'm sad

yes, but I can't talk to you because it costs $2 a minute
(I only have a cell phone now)
I'm sorry

ok well
give it to me
but you don't like

I tried to call you on my computer

should I call you
yes or no

but it didn't work

```
yes I have
the same
cell phone
try another day
```

well, it didn't work. I'll try again
I don't have a home phone, I'm telling you, only a cell
phone that's not for international calls

```
and how is your family
```

ok—not so good

```
but I can call you
```

I was helping my mom for a few months
no, it doesn't matter. it doesn't work.
(I know you don't believe me. fine.)

```
I think you have to buy another
international
cell phone
```

one day I will have a normal telephone

```
ayaaaaaa
yes because from here it's also very
expensiveeeeeee
```

but you know….i don't like talking on the telephone

```
haha
ok
```

ayaaaaaa

thank you for the conversation, it was a great pleasure

but there you can say sweet things
live life don't let life live you.
surfing lo mejor en galapagos ;)
when is your birthday

good luck with the surfing competition
November 25th

ok
mine june 12th
thank you for the cap
I like it a lot
how did you know I'd like it

you're welcome, querido….haha it looks like the flags on your walls

yes thank you
for everything
I hope
to have a flag
for my room
I think you will come back
when you're already famous
from your book

oh, yeah? haha we'll see.

and you have enough money
yes of course

and what will you be doing?
you will have your own store, right?

what I'm always doing
yes of course
you know
what my dream is
to be manager

until later, querido.

you're going
ok
I have to eat a little
I hope you are well

rice, no

in everything

thank you
take good care of yourself

chicken and rice
and pizza
I invite you
let's go

byee

ok
if you can call me
amorcitooooo
lejanooooo
you will be
always
chaoooooooo

Bibliography

Bartolomé, Luis, ed. *Guía Total: Ecuador Islas Galápagos*. Madrid: Grupo Ayana, S.A., 2000.

Beyond the Gates of Splendor. Dir. Jim Hanon. 2002. DVD. 20th Century Fox, 2005.

Cabodevilla, Miguel Angel. *Oro Creciente y Otros Relatos de Selva Adentro*. Quito: CICAME, 1998.

Cabodevilla, Miguel Angel. *El Exterminio de los Pueblos Ocultos*. Quito: CICAME, 2004.

Coperthwaite, William S. *A Handmade Life*. Vermont: Chelsea Green, 2003.

Elliot, Elisabeth. *Through Gates of Splendor*. New York: Harper, 1957.

Elliot, Elisabeth. *The Savage, My Kinsman*. New York: Harper and Brothers, 1961.

End of the Spear. Dir. Jim Hanon. 2006. DVD. 20th Century Fox, 2006.

Eviatar, Daphne. "The High Cost of Oil." *The Nation*. Vol. 281, No. 4. Aug 1-Aug 8, 2005: 26+.

Foreman, Tom. "Anthropologist on Living with a Remote Amazon Tribe." *Inside Base Camp*. National Geographic News, http://www.nationalgeographic.com. Interview with Dr. Flora Lu Holt, May 21, 2003.

Gartelmann, Karl Dieter. *El Mundo Perdido de los Aucas*. Quito: Imprenta Mariscal, 1977.

"'Go Ye and Preach the Gospel:' Five Do and Die." *LIFE Magazine*. Vol. 40, No. 5. January 30, 1956: 10–19.

Kane, Joe. *Savages*. New York: Knopf, 1995.

Keep the River on Your Right: A Modern Cannibal Tale. Dir. Laurie Gwen Shapiro, David Shapiro. 2000. DVD. New Video Group, 2002.

Man, John. *Jungle Nomads of Ecuador: The Waorani*. Amsterdam: Time-Life, 1982.

Marcella, Gabriel and Richard Downes, ed. *Security Cooperation in the Western Hemisphere: Resolving the Ecuador-Peru Conflict*. Miami: North South Center Press, 1999.

Maxus Ecuador, Inc. "Bleeding Heart of Darkness." *Harper's Magazine*. Vol. 289, Issue 1733, October 1994: 20–21.

Patzelt, Erwin. *Los Huaorani: Los Ultimos Hijos Libres del Jaguar*. Quito: Banco Central del Ecuador, 2002.

Rival, Laura M. *Trekking Through History: The Huaorani of Amazonian Ecuador*. New York: Columbia University Press, 2002.

Rival, Laura M. *Hijos del Sol, Padres del Jaguar: Los Huaorani de Ayer y Hoy*. Quito, Ecuador: Ediciones Abya-Yala, 1996.

Rival, Laura M. "Ecuador: The Huaorani People of the Amazonia, Self-isolation and Forced Contact." *World Rainforest Movement Bulletin*. No. 87, October 2004.

Robarchek, Clayton A. and Carole J. Robarcheck. "Trinkets and Beads." *American Anthropologist*. Vol. 100, No. 4, Dec. 1998: 1016–1017.

Robarchek, Clayton Allen. *Waorani: the Contexts of Violence and War*. Fort Worth: Harcourt Brace, 1998.

Robarchek, Clayton A. and Carole J. Robarchek. "Cultures of War and Peace: A Comparative Study of Waorani and Semai." In *Aggression and Peacefulness in Humans and Other Primates*. L. Gray and J. Silverberg, eds. New York: Oxford University Press, 1992.

Rousseau, J.J. *Discourse on the Origin and Foundations of Inequality among Men*. 1755. Trans. Franklin Philip. Oxford: Oxford University Press, 1994.

Saint, Stephen E. "The Unfinished Mission to the 'Aucas.'" *Christianity Today*. Vol. 42 No. 3, March 2, 1998: 42–45.

Saltos, Cecilia Viera. *Ecuador en Guerra 1995*. Guayaquil: Publicaciones de Interés Social.

Sandall, Roger. *The Culture Cult: Designer Tribalism and Other Essays*. Boulder, Colorado: Westview Press, 2001.

Schneebaum, Tobias. *Keep the River on your Right*. New York: Grove Press, 1982.

Sinclair, Andrew. *The Naked Savage*. London: Sinclair-Stevenson, 1991.

Sinclair, Andrew. *The Savage: a history of misunderstanding*. London: Weidenfeld and Nicolson, 1977.

Smith, Randy. *Crisis Under the Canopy*. Quito: Abya-Yala, 1993.

Tagliani, Lino. *También el Sol Muere: Cuatro Años con los Huaorani*. Ecuador: Ediciones CICAME, 2004.

Torgovnick, Marianna. *Primitive Passions*. Chicago: University of Chicago Press, 1998.

Tylor, Edward Burnett. *Anthropology: An Introduction to the Study of Man and Civilizaton*. London: Macmillan and Co., 1881.

Villalta, Blanco. *Ritos Caníbales en América*. Buenos Aires: Casa Pardo, 1970.

Walton, Priscilla L. *Our Cannibals, Ourselves*. Chicago: U. of Illinois Press, 2004.

Warren, Adrian. "Waorani: The Last People." *BBC Wildlife Magazine*. Vol. 2, No. 9, September 1984: 454–457.

Wood, Rick. "Fighting Dependency Among 'the Aucas:' An Interview with Steve Saint." *Mission Frontiers Bulletin*, May–June 1998: 9–14.

Yost, James A. "Twenty Years of Contact: the Mechanisms of Change in Huao ('Auca') culture." In Norman E. Whitten, Jr., ed. *Cultural Transformations and Ethnicity in Modern Ecuador*. Champaign-Urbana: University of Illinois Press, 1981: 677–704.

Yost, James A. "People of the Forest: The Waorani." In *Ecuador: All'Ombra dei Vulcani*. Venice: Casa Editrice Erizzo, 1981: 95–115.

Ziegler-Otero, Lawrence. *Resistance in an Amazonian Community: Huaorani OrganizingAgainst the Global Economy*. New York: Berghahn, 2004.

About the Author

Carla Seidl studied at Harvard University, where she created her own major called Expression and Culture Studies. She has traveled extensively, speaks several languages, and served as a Peace Corps Volunteer in Azerbaijan from 2006 to 2008. Carla is also an emerging singer-songwriter and independent radio producer. Read and hear samples of her latest work at www.carlaseidl.com.

CPSIA information can be obtained
at www.ICGtesting.com
Printed in the USA
BVHW030248121019
560940BV00001B/49/P